About the Author

Born in Finglas, north Dublin, in 1959, Dermot Bolger is one of Ireland's best known writers. His twelve novels include *The Journey Home*, *Father's Music*, *The Valparaiso Voyage*, *The Family on Paradise Pier*, *A Second Life*, *New Town Soul*, *The Fall of Ireland* and *Tanglewood*.

His first play, *The Lament for Arthur Cleary*, received the Samuel Beckett Award. His numerous other plays include *The Ballymun Trilogy*, which charts forty years of life in a Dublin working-class suburb; a stage adaptation of James Joyce's *Ulysses*; *Walking the Road*, about the life of Francis Ledwidge; *In High Germany*, which was filmed by RTÉ television, and its sequel – twenty years on – *The Parting Glass*.

His first collection of poems, *The Habit of Flesh*, was published in 1980 and his ninth collection, *The Venice Suite: A Voyage Through Loss*, appeared in 2012. As an eighteen-year-old factory hand, Bolger founded Raven Arts Press, which he ran until its closure in 1992.

He devised the best-selling collaborative novels, *Finbar's Hotel* and *Ladies Night at Finbar's Hotel* and has edited numerous anthologies, including *The Picador Book of Contemporary Irish Fiction*. A former Writer Fellow at Trinity College, Dublin and Playwright in Association with the Abbey Theatre, Bolger writes for most of Ireland's leading newspapers and in 2012 was named Commentator of the Year at the Irish Newspaper Awards.

www.dermotbolger.com

D0417259

Praise for Dermot Bolger

'Bolger's vision of the city is ragingly incandescent ... in some senses Bolger is to contemporary Dublin what Dickens was to Victorian London: archivist, reporter, sometimes infuriated lover. Certainly no understanding of Ireland's capital is complete without an acquaintance with his magnificent writing.'
— Joseph O'Connor, *Books Quarterly*, USA

'Joyce, O'Flaherty, Brian Moore, John McGahern, a fistful of O'Brien's. This is a succulent Who's Who of Irish Writing, and Dermot Bolger is of the same ilk ... an exceptional literary gift.'
— *Independent* (London)

'Fierce, fierce work, dark, passionate and cathartic. Unique, strangely elegiac and loving. And the new poems are just astounding.'
— Sebastian Barry

'I think of Bolger as Dublin's Pasolini or, conversely, of Pasolini as Rome's Bolger. Bolger's poems are Dublin Elegies to lay alongside the Roman Elegies of Pasolini. And then there are other times when I think of Dermot Bolger as the Francis Ledwidge who has survived the war, married and had children, and now is reporting the whole story back to us in sequences of heartbreaking poems. Like Ledwidge, Bolger is a direct, lineal descendant of John Keats; he writes out of "the holiness of the heart's affections".'
— Paul Durcan

Praise for *The Venice Suite*

'"In the numbness of grief I felt certain I would never write poems again," Bolger claims in his prefatory note. But his readers will be glad that he has done so ... [in] ... what is ultimately a book of celebration ... unflinching and sad – and beautiful.'

– *Times Literary Supplement*

'These are moving and wonderful poems of inclusion and remembrance. The entire collection works as a marvellous elegy. Grief is called up and colours everything Bolger does with his technical excellence. Heartbreaking.'

– Thomas McCarthy, *Irish Examiner*

Also by Dermot Bolger

Poetry
The Habit of Flesh
Finglas Lilies
No Waiting America
Internal Exiles
Leinster Street Ghosts
Taking My Letters Back
The Chosen Moment
External Affairs
The Venice Suite

Novels
Night Shift
The Woman's Daughter
The Journey Home
Emily's Shoes
A Second Life
Father's Music
Temptation
The Valparaiso Voyage
The Family on Paradise Pier
The Fall of Ireland
Tanglewood

Young Adult Novel
New Town Soul

Collaborative Novels
Finbar's Hotel
Ladies Night at Finbar's Hotel

Plays
The Lament for Arthur Cleary
Blinded by the Light
In High Germany
The Holy Ground
One Last White Horse
April Bright
The Passion of Jerome
Consenting Adults
The Ballymun Trilogy
1. From These Green Heights
2. The Townlands of Brazil
3. The Consequences of Lightning
Walking the Road
The Parting Glass
Tea Chests & Dreams

Editor
The Picador Book of Contemporary Irish Fiction (UK)
The Vintage Book of Contemporary Irish Fiction (USA)

That Which Is
Suddenly Precious

New & Selected Poems

Dermot Bolger

NEW ISLAND

THAT WHICH IS SUDDENLY PRECIOUS

First published in 2015 by
New Island Books
16 Priory Hall Office Park
Stillorgan
County Dublin
Republic of Ireland

www.newisland.ie

Copyright © Dermot Bolger, 2015

The author has asserted his moral rights.

PRINT ISBN: 978-1-84840-469-4
EPUB ISBN: 978-1-84840-470-0
MOBI ISBN: 978-1-84840-471-7

British Library Cataloguing Data.
A CIP catalogue record for this book is available from the British Library.

Front cover image of author at work in the Raven Arts offices in 1980, courtesy of Leo Duffy.
Back cover image © Peter O'Doherty and courtesy of Peter O'Doherty.

Typeset by JVR Creative India
Cover design by Mariel Deegan
Printed by SPRINT-print Ltd., Dublin

10 9 8 7 6 5 4 3 2 1

Acknowledgements

These poems were written between 1975 and 2015. Sincere thanks to the editors of numerous newspapers, magazines, radio programmes and anthologies where many of them first appeared.

'Ballymun Incantation' was recited by actors and locals in a performance directed by Ray Yeates as the centrepiece of a public wake on the eve of the demolition of the first high-rise tower block in Ballymun in 2004.

'Travel-Light' was read by the actor Vincent McCabe at the opening of the Dublin Port Tunnel in 2007.

'Night in the House on Dawson Street' received its first public reading by the actors Barry McGovern and Geraldine Plunkett, directed by Mark O'Brien, as the centrepiece of an evening in Dublin's Mansion House in 2015, which marked the 300th anniversary of the purchase of said house for the official residence of the Lord Mayor of Dublin.

'The Venice Suite' was read on RTÉ Radio by the actor John Kavanagh in a performance directed and produced by Aidan Matthews in 2013.

'The Stolen Future', reproduced as a Giclee print, forms part of an exhibition created and curated by Larry Lambe in which artists respond to the 100th anniversary of the Easter Rising.

'Blind Golf' was read by the author on the occasion of the ISPS Handa Irish Blind Golf Open Championship, 2014, staged by the Irish Blind Golf Society, of which the author is a patron.

'The Frost is All Over' sequence was performed with interlinked tunes played by two superb musicians: accordion player Tony McMahon and uilleann piper David Power. Sincere thanks to David Teevan who put this stage show together.

Thanks to Leo Duffy for permission to use, on the front cover of this book, his photograph of me at work in the Raven Arts offices in 1980, and to Peter O'Doherty for permission to use, on the back cover, his photograph of me on stage three and a half decades later.

Finally, my sincere thanks to everyone involved in New Island for seeing *That Which Is Suddenly Precious* into print.

In gratitude to all those, living and dead, who have been with me, and who continue to be with me, on the journey charted within this book.

Contents

In Memory of my Cousin, Geraldine Kelly (2015)   1

From *The Habit of Flesh* (1980)
The Road Ledwidge Walked   7
Having Never Run Away   8
The Lady in the Fields   9

From *Finglas Lilies* (1981)
Finglas Lilies   13
Aisling Fionn Ghlas   15
Captain of a Space Ship   17

From *No Waiting America* (1982)
Ontario Terrace, Rathmines   21
Dreams of Glass   22
Stardust Sequence   23

From *A New Primer for Irish Schools* (1985)
Renunciation   29
Lullaby of a Woman of the Flats   30
The Children of 1966   31
'Bob Marley Lives'   33
Dublin Girl, Mountjoy Jail, 1984   34
Snuff Movies   35

From *Internal Exiles* (1986)
Bluebells for Grainne   39
The Watcher's Agony:
    1. The Ghosts in the Ark   40
    2. The Watcher's Agony   41
Matt Talbot   42
The Lament for Arthur Cleary   43

From *Leinster Street Ghosts* (1989)
The Buried Stream   59
Leinster Street Ghosts   60
Owen   66
A Memory of Madeleine Stuart   69
Beechwood Avenue   70
Wishbone   72
Leinster Street   73

From *Taking My Letters Back* (1998)
Prayer   77
Wherever You Woke   78
Lines for an Unknown Uncle   79
April Bright   80
Poem Found in a Faded Newspaper   81
Algae Hibernicae   83
Polygonum Baldschuanicum   85
Ireland, 1967   86
Taking My Letters Back   87
'Last Songs' by Francis Ledwidge   89
Going Home for Christmas   90
Martha   91
In Memory of Rory Gallagher   92
Temple Street Children's Hospital   93
Ash Wednesday   95
Millbourne Avenue, Winter   96
Holotropic Botanicus   97
On a Train in England   98
Three Seasons For My Sons   99
   – Walking on a Spring Evening with My Two Sons   101
   – Collecting Chestnuts with My Sons, September, 1995 102
   – The Constellations of Drumcondra   104

From *The Chosen Moment* (2004)
The Chosen Moment   109
The Brigadier   110
Drumcondra Bridge   111
A Poet of the 1950s   112
At Twenty   113
A Steep Lane in Monaghan   114
Remembering Certain Golf Holes   115
Absent Friends   116
Approaching My 45th Birthday   117
Let There Be Space   118
Strangers   119
After The Chase   120
Letters Sent Back in 19th Century Copies of *The Annals for
    Propagation of the Faith*, Abandoned in the Attics of All Hallows
    Seminary   121
The Baily Lighthouse   123
The Former Lady Golf Captain   124
Verses Put Aside Between My 40th and 41st Birthday   126

From *External Affairs* (2008)
Ballymun Incantation   133
Travel-Light   136
In Memory of George Best   138
Carmen's Garden in Flanders   139
First Book   140
The Cut   141

From *Night & Day: 24 Hours in the Life of Dublin* (2008)
Author's Note to *Night and Day*   144
On the 7 a.m. Luas to Tallaght   145
Conquistador, Pilgrim Soul   146
History Viewed from a Clondalkin Supermarket Car Park   148
Neilstown Matadors   149
Girl, Fifteen, Walking in Ronanstown   151
Graffiti on a Corner   152
Wedded   153
The Absent Father   155
Passing Certain Housing Estates   156
Flowers Mark the Spot   157
Haulier passing The Red Cow Roundabout, 11.15 p.m.   158
Jesus of Clondalkin   159
Possibility   160

From *The Frost Is All Over* Suite (2007)
Tuning Up   163
'Culna Dear, Don't Come Any Nearer Me…'   164
Seamus Ennis in Drumcondra   165
Recording   167
Bold Doherty   168
'O'Neill's Cavalcade'   169
Sport   170
Sonny Brogan's Jigs   171
The Piper Patsy Touhey plays in Cohen's Variety Show,
    New York, 1905   173
The Frost is All Over   174
'O'Neill's Music of Ireland'   176
The Nomad   177

From *The Venice Suite* (2012)
Author's Note to The Venice Suite   181
Venice   187
Jack B. Yeats's Painting, *Grief* (1951)   189
The Empty Car   190
Fingal Driving Range   192
Warmth   193
Lines Transcribed from Latvian   195
That Which is Suddenly Precious…   196
Candle   198
So Many First Times…   200
Little Xs   201
Other People's Grief   203
Christmas Eve, 2010   204
The Final Three Words   206
Where We Are Now   209
While We Sleep   212

New Poems (2013–2015)
Night in the House on Dawson Street   217
The Stolen Future   223
'Whatever Happened To Francis Stable?'   226
Blind Golf   227

In Memory of my Cousin, Geraldine Kelly

Nobody again will ever be lowered into this grave.
In time nobody will stand here, where I first stood

At the age of seven, having walked with my mother
Through Finglas Wood to enter these cemetery gates

As evening light faded along avenues of scripted stone
Down which we wandered, guided only by her memory

To the grave holding the remains of her sister Maureen.
The bare plot was unmarked. All my mother had to steer by

Was her sense of injustice that an in-law had erected no stone
Or makeshift cross to help his wife's people locate her resting place.

People's names become their final possession, yet in this necropolis,
Maureen Kelly, née Flanagan, had no chiselled proof of identity.

As twilight enveloped us, my mother and I hastened to the gates
Of this graveyard where, three years later, she was also interred.

Maureen died four months after my birth. Geraldine. In that upheaval
You became segregated behind high walls of hospitals and convents.

Crushed by the impossibility of raising a Down's syndrome daughter
On his own, your father ceded your care to nuns in butterfly cornettes.

I don't know enough about this burdened widower to speak for him.
I sense only how certain lives seem blighted by a contagion of miasma;

I know he did all he could for you, taking you home for weekend visits
To his house where, overcome by illness, he fell into an open fire

Which scorched his features while you watched, shaking with fright,
Too scared to assist him or articulate the terror flooding your heart.

In time high walls dissipate under fresh thinking and fire regulations.
No longer hidden from sight, you were chaperoned into a cosseted world

Where you found companionship. With most cousins scattered abroad,
Open-hearted fellow residents in sheltered bungalows became your kin,

Surrogate siblings amongst whom you felt comfortable enough
To shed your timid shyness, to joke and tease and become again

The joyous free spirit who used to wake your cousin June at dawn
By dancing on her bed which you shared during childhood visits,

Back when you were oblivious to your mother's illness, the tumour
Eroding Maureen's sight as she struggled to maintain a vegetable shop

In Parnell Street, where some locals slyly robbed a dying woman blind.
How did they explain loss to a child seemingly destined never to grow up?

But grow up you did, gaining confidence in the confines of care homes
That offered sanctuary and kinship but rendered your life invisible

To most outsiders except the cousin whose childhood bed you shared.
June brought you for days out to Malahide, her children around you

As you fed swans from a rocking jetty on the Broadmeadows estuary,
Shyly displayed your paintings, coaxed notes from a piano and relaxed,

Momentarily reintegrated into this wider family you never truly knew.
But eventually you no longer even recognized June, having lived longer

Than either of your parents, longer than my mother who once minded you.
Alzheimer's became the last of many barriers that separated you from us.

But just once, allow me to weave you back into our patchwork of lineage,
Into the tapestry of second cousins who may not be aware of your name.

Let me grasp your hands in mine and swing you breathlessly in dizzy circles
Backwards through time till you break my grip and land. Look around you:

It is an august morning in 1934. Six carefree sisters laugh as they run
In summer frocks up the steep lane that leads to their farmhouse home,

All dreaming of the future, yet all still unburdened by their futures,
Teasing one another about boys, absorbed in the unnoticed wonder

Of teetering on the astounding cusp that is the verge of womanhood.
Two older brothers wave to them from a sloping field of ripened barley,

Their elderly father sitting out in the yard, greets them as they race
To climb onto a five-barrel gate, leaning back to swing upside-down,

Shining hair cascading downwards, hands keeping their frocks upright
As they survey sun-drenched childhood fields from this peculiar angle

Where everything is topsy-turvy and yet life has never seemed so clear
Than in this swaying communion of sisterhood, laughter and belonging

In which they gaze towards a horizon so blue in the forenoon heat haze
That they cannot see us approach. All they can sense in their closeness

Is the panting breath of each sister, each heartbeat loud in this stillness
Where they survey the homestead they must leave for the cities in which

Their essence is continually reborn in granddaughters and great-grandsons;
In the lips of Michelle and Deirdre, the countenance of Joseph and Mairead;

3

In Maureen's laugh that lived on inside your own, Geraldine; in the smile
Of Roger and Tony, of Ciara and Joan, of Linda, Stephen and Sinead,

In the features of Jonah and Flynn, of Fiona and Clare, of Romy and Ava;
The eyes of Donnacha and Diarmuid; in the eyes of Jamie, in eyes of Jade.

April 2015

From *The Habit of Flesh*
(1980)

The Road Ledwidge Walked

Leaving your cottage on the North Road
We met a friend, a drunken student
Hitching through the night to Kilshane Cross.
He called Yeats a fascist. We argued at 3 a.m.
Where the final streetlight yielded to darkness.

When he was gone, I found a Royal Mail milestone
Placed here a century ago. I realised how Ledwidge
Had paused there to rest during his walk home
To Slane at sixteen: the night he left his city job,
Confused and excited after writing his first poem.

Choosing my own route past the garage and shops
I recalled the mythic creatures who wandered
His woods, populated by fawns and silver birds,
But who took flight when I wrote about reality,
Sexual desire and death: such dirty words.

Finglas, 1975

Having Never Run Away

I

Having never run away from home,
I could only imagine the strain
    Of hiding beneath some hedgerow
Lit by a single street-lamp down a lane:
    My school bag a makeshift pillow
As I read comics smudged by the rain.

My mother would anxiously wait
For a rescuer to carry me in triumph
    Into the bustling police station
Where she would cradle my head:
    All quarrels resolved as I returned
To the sanctuary of my warm bed.

II

Tonight I walk home
From some hazy party:
The streets freeze,
Leaves blow past me.

The house is empty.
I search for a light switch
And realise that home
Has run away from me.

1975

The Lady in the Fields

For Sheila Fitzgerald

I

The first night in your caravan I screamed
    And woke in unaccustomed dark,
Listening to the sounds across the fields
    Of wind and cattle and a dog's bark.

Your breakfast table grew cluttered
    As books and memories laid siege
To the food that we forgot to eat,
    As we rocked in tides of the breeze.

We startled foxes in your forest sanctuary
    In which aloof in-laws once presided
Over a Big House, where tangled vines now
    Invade rooms whose floors have subsided.

That night we spoke by candlelight,
    Sipping Lemon Balm scented tea,
Till dawn broke the hymen of night
    And we confided secrets effortlessly.

At half six we woke in heavy rain
    To the cries of a mutilated cat,
Who instinctively crawled to your door
    After being struck by a truck.

You gathered him in your arms,
    To finger each shattered bone,
And guided him to a peaceful death,
    Tenderly administering chloroform.

While I dug a grave in the field
   You laid him in an old blanket,
And said you would stop having pets,
   There was too much suffering in it.

II

   Thank you for your letter.
You say the snow has finally gone,
   The moon is so orange and full,
Transforming your field into an Eden.

   Four cats live in a basket
And respect songbirds that come,
   And live with sheep who rub
Thick winter coats against your door.

   In the frozen dawn food appears
For all your sheltering friends,
   Who seek you out with wounds
That your empathy slowly mends.

   Unbowed veteran of tragedy,
Defiant embracer of happiness:
   In your quest for simplicity,
You have stripped back your life

   To its essential essence
Of radiance, a single welcoming light,
   That shines amid dark fields:
A tiny ark beckoning us in the night.

1978

From *Finglas Lilies* (1981)

Finglas Lilies

I: Finglas, June 1977

A girl lies in the grass,
Beyond the lights of the party:
    Dew soaking her dress.

Flocks of leaves swarm
Above them like water lilies
    Adorning an ornate pond.

Each deep arousing kiss
Brims with giddy intoxication
    As they savour the bliss

Of futures stretching ahead:
Exams finished, adult possibilities
    More alluring than any caress.

Then panic pushes them apart,
As he withdraws from her too late.
    They lie scared, hands clasped.

II: London, Autumn 1977

A tiny flat in West London,
    They live on frozen food,
Make friends across the landing.

At night she often cries.
    They make love softly
For fear of harming the child

13

Developing like a negative
   In the pit of her stomach.
They finally call her relatives.

On the night crossing Dublin rose
   Like a curtain over a window
With thousands of bullet holes.

   III: Finglas, March 1979

Steel winds at dawn sting like a wasp,
   In this factory where men curse
And rust grows like hair on a corpse.

She's off to work as he finishes night shift.
   Today is their child's first birthday,
They'll put his name on the housing list.

Taking a chair he sits in the garden,
   Smoking Moroccan dope and tripping,
The housing estate keeps disappearing.

He feels that he is at the bottom of a pond
   Floating below rows of water lilies
With new names like Finglas and Ballymun.

Aisling Fionn Ghlas

One morning with sunlight
　　　You burst upon my life,
In your brother's house,
　　　Crashing there for the night.

His door creaking open,
　　　Hands searching for gloves,
The snap-shock of waking,
　　　To glimpse you, my love.

From his window I watched
　　　You move, so compact,
Your slender body tightened
　　　Up by the act

Of bending down to tie
　　　A small dog's rein,
At fifteen, in taut jeans,
　　　In a Finglas lane.

In a factory in England
　　　On night-shift, looking back,
I'd remember your body emerging
　　　From that cul-de-sac

Reflected by the steel moon
　　　In a guttered pool of rain,
Your smile over my machine
　　　Marked morning again.

Gentle as a Japanese lady,
      With slow dignity,
Pregnant for the third time,
      Two years married:

I called your name by the shops
      The day I came home,
Your smile when you turned
      Was bathed in Valium.

1980

Captain of a Space Ship

For Tom Casey, poet of the Ballymun towers

'I pace upon the battlements and stare.' – W. B. Yeats

Below concrete clouds,
On a level with my eyes,
    The seagulls cry
With white electric noise.

    I watch from the balcony
Of a high-rise tower block
    Roads quiet as veins
When blood has stopped.

It's freezing at this hour
    As I huddle in my coat,
Captain of a space ship
    Which never got afloat.

When the first bus moves
    From its terminus,
Sweet God of Morning
    Look down over us

Who watch from balconies
    As cars, lane by lane,
Speed towards distant offices
    Past this fertility farm,

Or lovers skip school,
    Flitting into back fields
Beyond the estates
    To flirt and smoke hash.

I sent them the love
    Of these seventy years,
But it's my experience
    That I wish to share.

At my table all night
    I tried to find words
For the wounds of Liverpool
    To somehow be cured,

Or doss houses in Glasgow,
    Or drying out in The Smoke.
I fed them my life-story,
    But the words never spoke.

My poems are neon bulbs
    In an underpass at night,
People walking to work
    Barely see them in dawn light.

On those in their frustration
    Who smash at each bulb
See how the splinters of glass
    Bear the imprint of blood.

1980

From *No Waiting America*
(1982)

Ontario Terrace, Rathmines

TO LOVE YOU is to be in love with everything.
The whole city blurs into streamlets of colour,

Then realigns into blue tar and grained concrete.
White and amber street lights dissipate at dawn,

Where canal locks grit their teeth and gurgle
With tired green water that sprays itself asunder.

To love you is to roll up these dawn-lit streets
And carry them home as photographs in a wallet.

6 February 1982

Dreams of Glass

INSIDE MY DREAM we were thrown together,
But segregated by all our private fears
That we were each afraid to tell the other.
When we went to touch we found ourselves
On opposite sides of a sheet of glass,
Our flesh pressed against the cold pane.

And I became a terrified black bird
Hurling myself against the glass partition,
Croaking out one tiny shrill word:
'Open! Open!' My heart thumping
Inside that body of feathers and down,
Frantically trying to gain your attention.

I want to nest in your arms and shelter
When the last train echoes down the tracks
To seal night-time into the silence after:
The fish nosing up the ice-blocked river,
The one who finds you, bleeding but alive,
In the charred ruins of the city after surrender.

1981

Stardust Sequence

In memory of the forty-eight young people killed by fire in the Stardust
Nightclub, Artane, North Dublin, 1982.

I

SHADOWS WHISPER a new language of possibilities
From hidden couples reminding us we are not alone
In searching for romance and the shared kindship
Of dancing to the beat and rhythm of our peers.
Through steel shutters clamped across emergency exits
Rock music invents a vocabulary that unites ours.

Strobe lights on the ceiling distort the air until
The brain keeps pace with the body's theatricality
In a flickering, disjointed black-and-white movie.
Every Friday friends gather to mingle and dance
In exhilarating tempo until the harsh glare of lights
Evicts you from a space you briefly felt was yours.

Thrust out into the night you'd doss or go home
Among couples & groups of girls singing love songs.
But tomorrow you will wander incubator estates
And stare disbelieving, in the brutality of dawn,
At silent families maintaining vigils in doorways
With only numb anger left burning inside them.

II

LAST NIGHT in swirling colour we danced again,
And, as strobe lights stunned in black & white,
I reached in this agony of slow motion for you.
But you danced on as if cold light still shone,
Merging into the crowd as my path was blocked
By snarling bouncers & dead-eyed club owners.

When I screamed across the music nobody heard,
I flailed under spotlights like a disco dancer
And people formed a circle, clapping to the beat
As I shuddered round the club in a violent fit,
Hurtling through a dream without tumbling awake,
I revolved through space until I hit the ground.

Lying among their feet tramping out the tunes,
I grasped you inside my mind for this moment,
Your white dress bobbing in a cool candle-flame,
Illuminating the darkness spinning towards me:
A teenage dancing queen, proud of her footwork,
Sparks rising like stardust all over the floor.

III

WE LIVE here on the edge of people's memories,
A reference point in the calendar of their lives.
Our absence linked with acceptances or refusals
On summer evenings when love seemed attainable
And eager lips opened after dances in the parks.
We are the unavoidable stillbirth of your past.

That golden girl you loved, pregnant at seventeen;
Young friends growing sour, paralysed by the dole;
Your senile boss, already rotting inside his skin,
Returns the look of hatred that's burning you up,
Drawing new breath from every young life wrecked.
All those smooth men who would quietly forget us,

Who turn you on a spit over cold flames of dissent,
Are guilty of murder as if they chained the fire exits
When we stampeded through their illusion of order.
We have buried in your skull these ashes of doubt
And you believe in nothing but one slow fuse of anger
Since the night your thin candle of youth ran out.

1982

From *A New Primer for Irish Schools* (1985)

Renunciation

After P. H. Pearse's poem, 'Renunciation'

Naked I saw thee, sweet beauty beyond beauty,
    But I blinded my eyes for fear I would fail;
My palms were dry and my raked body shivering,
    When I screamed awake from her teasing laughter.

      no longer can I feel my face under this second skin:
          they have fused together under rain and baked in the heat
      of platforms where my voice invented a nation to live in,
          among haunted eyes staring from the faces of defeat.

Christ, I see Thee in Thy rituals and certainty,
    Shield me in the confines of Your lonely march;
My mind knows the fever of a barefoot boy's kiss,
    Let the wafer of Your manliness slacken my thirst.

      armed men believe I command them, but they lead me
          out of myself, into this role where I may express,
      by a million doves of flame released over the town,
          how, when the heart cannot open, it must burn down.

1983

Lullaby of a Woman of the Flats

After P. H. Pearse's poem, 'Lullaby of a Woman of the Mountains'

Small fragile head, my life's precious candle,
I will guard your sleep before longings claim you.

Smeared hungry mouth that my breast has known,
You will be tempted by the milk of heroin and flour.

Flushed crimson checks, before stubble can harden,
Apostles of violence will brand their caste onto you.

Powdered milk of death besieging my baby's mouth,
This city's ashen hands anointing his cheeks!

Flats, be still, and insatiable hungers that gnaw
Stay banished inside your lair of television tubes.

Cars, below the balconies, deaden your engines,
Brandished flick-knives silence your beckoning.

Siren and gunshot, do not echo through my home,
Chords of wanderlust do not taunt him to come.

Phantoms of our age that call in the night-time,
Do not stir tonight till cursed streets whiten.

1984

The Children of 1966

An ordered ocean of flags swaying at dawn,
We shall march forth to meet with destiny.

Gold banners between houses in every town,
We shall march forth to meet with destiny.

Their medals glinting in the ageing ranks,
The survivors marched past their monuments,
Faces proud and stiff in each camera lens:
We shall march forth to meet with destiny.

An ordered sea of feet among littered bread,
We shall march forth to meet with destiny.

Gulls shriek as teachers drill us into step,
We shall march forth to meet with destiny.

We paraded in line between wooden desks,
Past a framed proclamation and a crucifix,
And begged God that our turn would be next:
We shall march forth to meet with destiny.

A tide of rhetoric flooding the platforms,
We shall march forth to meet with destiny.

Engraining a call to duty into our bones,
We shall march forth to meet with destiny.

Images of trapped men racing through flames
Left the incomplete ache of a phantom pain,
But through our blood they would be freed
When we marched forth to meet with destiny.

We would march forth to meet with destiny.

1996

'Bob Marley Lives'

The wall by the fire station bears your legend
    In scrawled metallic red lettering,

And young girls converging in the park at dusk
    Listen to your Jamaican voice singing.

I cross the arched skeleton of a pedestrian bridge
    Where lads with guitars strum

And under glistening dreadlocks of a burst main
    Children race in wild abandon,

With the pulse of your music threading every vein
    Of our new nation being born,

As you help us still to sing songs of freedom,
    On Finglas streets, redemption songs.

1985

Dublin Girl, Mountjoy Jail, 1984

I dreamt it all: from end to end, the carriageway,
The rivulet behind the dairy streaked with crystal,
A steel moon glinting in a guttered stream of rain,
And the steep hill that I would crest to find her:
My child asleep in my old bedroom beside my sister.

I dreamt it all: and when I woke, furtive girls
Were clambering onto the bars on the windows,
White shapes waving against the dark skyline,
Praying for hands to reply from the men's cells
Before screws broke up our vigil of handkerchiefs.

I dreamt it all: the times I swore never again
To walk that carriageway, a tempest of heroin glowing
In my veins until I shivered in its aftertaste,
And hid with my child in the closed-down factory
Where my brain snapped like a brittle fingernail.

I dreamt it all: the longing to touch her, the séance
In the cell when we screamed at the picture falling,
The warmth of circled hands after the freezing glass
Between my child and me, a warder following her words
To be rationed out and lived off for days afterwards.

I dreamt of you, who means all to me, my daughter;
How we might run up that carriageway by the rivulet,
And, when I woke, a blue pupil was patrolling my sleep,
Jailing my dreams in the vacant orbit of its world:
Narrowed down to a spyhole, a globed eyelid closing.

1984

34

Snuff Movies

In Memory of Pier Paolo Pasolini

Wind rattles the window frames and the floorboards rot.
It's been eight days since I stepped beyond this filthy flat
Where I sit watching and four times my vigil was rewarded.

Four times I have hung within the limbo of static on the screen,
Longing for release, yet not daring to believe it could happen,
And four times the picture hasn't jerked back to advertisements:

My throat has turned dry and my hands trembled as I watched
The figure thrown naked into the room and the beating begin.
Whole days wither in this stagnant flat when nothing happens;

Days when I'm stuck like an insect on fly paper unable to move,
Trapped within cyberspace in a meteorite shower of static
Where I wait and pray that advertisements will not continue

As over and over they are repeated without commentary or pity,
Hammering out slogans at those remaining sealed in our rooms.
Once we walked down streets and worked in throbbing factories;

I remember oil on my overalls and the smell of sweat without fear,
But then governments collapsed, were reformed and then submerged
By corporations who quickly learnt how to function without us.

Just four times the knife has flashed like a matador's
And youngsters raised their heads, though blinded by the hood.
There's no way of knowing how many of my ex-workmates remain,

Caged before crackling screens, terrified to miss each murder.
Yesterday I saw a man with a plastic bag run through the litter:
Apart from him all streets were deserted to the superstore.

I breathe safely – I'm too old for anybody's attention,
They will never come to shove me hooded into a studio,
I won't strain my head forward in expectation of the blow.

From my final refuge I am allowed spy on their agony;
Their flesh wincing and their final anonymous pain.
Afterwards I breathe again in my renewed triumph of survival.

Nobody knows any longer when the curfew begins or ends
But one evening I heard them snatch someone on this street.
I never knew which hooded neighbour I had once passed

Kept the whole nation contained for a day with his death.
I know they are deliberately killing me too in this war of nerves:
It has been years since I've not slept sitting upright in a chair,

Dreaming of blood and waking fretfully to advertisements.
Yet still I cling on, speaking to nobody in the superstore,
Running home frantic that I will miss a final glimpse of life.

Long ago I believed in God – now I believe what I am told:
There is no heaven except the instant when the set comes alive,

No purgatory except infinite static bombarding the screen:
Hell could only be if they came for the television, or for me.

1983

From *Internal Exiles* (1986)

Bluebells for Grainne

Through the shuttered light of blinking trees we race,
Before the mobile library halts in a sleepy village
Where we climb down, light-headed from your farewell party,
For one final stop on the last day we will work together.

The old driver arranges flowers in the folds of your dress
As we laze against a sunlit wall, luxuriating in this afternoon
That stretches out like a kite we finger lightly to keep aloft,
Trailing its shimmering tails of our future dreams and hopes.

Often our brains felt baked by petty rules and regulations,
But we kept one another sane by learning how to sing
A subversive song of friendship which flowered underneath
This timetable that commands us to vanish in a swirl of dust.

When it settles, remember me, grinning idiotically up at you
In a spring dress, with bluebells spilling from your breast.

St Margaret's Village, 1984

The Watcher's Agony:
Two Poems

1. The Ghosts in the Ark

Just before we slept your tongue crept into my mouth.
I dreamt inside its aftertaste of a tide sifting out

And when I woke I was terrified you were taken from me,
I pressed against your body, waking you with my urgency.

The room above our heads became filled by the arms of men
From the foreign city you came from, forcing you down again.

Your body shuddered feeling mine, lost between two worlds,
And you gazed up at me, fearfully, not certain who I was.

In your eyes I could glimpse myself, exhausted and anxious,
But occluded from these memories that set adrift your brain.

The future balanced while I tried to quell your restiveness,
And, in my failure, the past crashed against our tiny ark.

Now each time you open yourself to love, old pain rushes in,
And ghosts hover like vultures, waiting to claim you back.

February 1983

2. The Watcher's Agony

The devil is in this room tonight. He wants us.
Cups rattle in your mind and the table levitates.

I hold on to your body as if trying to protect you,
But the terror trapped in your imagination escapes.

Can you hear one word I say or even feel my presence?
I cannot grasp what is disintegrating between my arms

Where you shudder, wedging yourself into my shoulder,
And then speak in a voice estranged from your own.

The devil is in this room tonight. Inside both of us:
Everything we ever suppressed attacks the furniture.

When I black out into sleep I dream I am still awake
And you lean above me, choking on words I cannot hear.

Your flat has broken loose from the moorings of reality,
It pitches and rolls through the tempest in your mind.

The devil you see, frantically tugging the smashed helm:
As he turns with wild eyes in the storm, is his face mine?

March 1983

Matt Talbot

1856–1925

I need to rinse out the rancid tin can you drank from
In a ramshackle shed beside the timber yard gates,

To place a mattress over the plank you slept on
And release rusted dog chains cutting into your flesh.

We have all sobered awake in the abyss of dawn,
Longing for a revelation to overwhelm our futility,

But you substituted masochism with an addict's fixation
That snared us in the obedient servitude of poverty.

Lift your head, Matt, and read on the newsboys' placards
How Dublin burns as you trudge each evening from work

To shuffle to your meal on bare knees across floorboards,
With blunt labourer's eyes outstaring all who would mock,

Until you fall in Granby Lane, missing your final Mass,
As if you carried the whole city's pain upon your back.

1986

The Lament for Arthur Cleary

Mo chara thú go daingean!
is níor chreideas riamh dod mharbh
gur tháinig chúgham do chapall
is a srianta léi go talamh,
is fuil do chroí ar a leacáin
　　From 'Caoineadh Airt Uí Laoghaire'
　　by Eibhlín Dubh Ní Chonaill (1770)

My lament for you, Arthur Cleary,
　As you lay down that crooked back lane,
Beneath the stern wall of a factory
　Where moss and crippled flowers cling

To stone crested by glass and wire,
　With a runlet of blood down your chest
When I raced screaming towards you,
　Hearing their clamour of boots retreat.

I cupped your face in my palms
　To taste life draining from your lips
And you died attempting to smile,
　As defiant and proud as you had lived.

Behind me I could hear the roar
　Of an engine kick-starting to life
And vanishing through laneways
　Where we had rode on autumn nights.

May it have led them mesmerised
  Beneath railway bridges to the river
And skidded over oily cobbles
  To drown those who killed its master.

You were the only man I knew,
  The rest were all dancing clones,
Lions swaggering in packs,
  Kittens petrified on their own,

Unable to glance at a girl
  Unless cocky with drink or stoned.
But you stared into my face,
  Caught in the strobe lights alone,

Not leering or smart-arsed,
  Nor mumbling like a blushing bride,
Leading me to the dance floor
  Where firm hands brushed my thighs.

Confettied light combed our faces
  From spinning globes of speckled mirrors
When we walked towards the exit
  Through those swirling ranks of dancers,

Beyond the cajoling disc jockey
  And nervous girls trying to look bored,
Away from the slow crucifixions
  I'd witnessed stranded on that dance floor.

Our ears still humming with static,
  We moved out into a tense nightscape,
Past the crumpled stalks of drunks
  Falling between the dispersed sheaves

Of crowds swept from discotheques;
   The glazed lovers with no place to stay
Queuing under the gaze of bouncers
   In O'Connell Street's honky-tonk cafes.

Sombre patriots and liberators
   Stood paralysed in bird-stained bronze
While you unchained your motor-bike,
   Handing me the only helmet to put on.

I accepted it like a pledge
   And my arms circled your leather jacket;
Your hair blown into my face,
   We raced up the quays towards my estate.

Down a lane choked with scrap,
   Littered by rust-eaten ghosts of lorries,
Within sight of my father's house
   Is where I first loved Arthur Cleary.

While jewels of shattered glass
   Sparkled in light from gypsy caravans,
I unpeeled my black sweater
   And my nipple hardened under his tongue.

Deserted streets had lightened
   Before I undressed in exhilaration,
And lay jaded beside my window
   To catch the first blue notes of dawn,

That blurred into whiteness
   Where he lay curled against my back,
His limbs clambering on top of me
   Until I woke by myself, sopping wet.

My lament for Arthur Cleary
   And the life that he tried to lead,
Taking what jobs suited him,
   Contemptuous of all permanency.

From the final generation
   To have always known a start
In factory or timber yard,
   Who moved on as work grew slack.

Those born in our new winter
   Are taught terror from birth
And moulded like Plasticine
   Into the first ensnaring niche,

Or are defeated early on
   By the propaganda of despair,
And chalk days off in blood
   On the city's dead-end corners.

They would run to the flats,
   Pursued by whirling sirens,
Rifling handbags plundered
   Through smashed car windows.

We ignored police questions
   And watched from your bike
The squad cars retreat
   And shaven heads strut out,

Tempted by a fraction
  Of the value from a fence:
White-socked tribesmen
  Shivering for their fix,

Their youth suffocated
  In the famine of poppies
That spread in the dust
  Blown down concrete steps,

With geriatric faces
  Screwed up in harsh light,
Watching for a dealer's car
  To slow at the entrance

And a hand to appear,
  Dispensing white packages
From a lowered window
  Before the driver accelerates.

I had a room with fresh linen
  And parents to watch over me,
A brown dog slept at my feet,
  I left them for Arthur Cleary.

To climb that steep aisle
  Scrawled with lovers' graffiti,
Where only genuflecting gulls
  Bore witness to our ceremony.

Flocks of children swarmed
  Along the cliff edge of doorways,
Women called to each other
  From balconies of swaying laundry

Above the blare of radios,
  Noise of soccer and girls laughing
On those honeycombed steps,
  Till dusk announced Friday evening

And furtive parents withdrew
  To sit in unlit rooms with children
Who waited, terrified to move,
  As the aggressive knocking began.

Behind walls we sensed them
  Like Jews hidden in compartments,
Hearing a moneylender's knuckles
  Scrape at their taut nerve ends.

                    *

Languid in its afterglow,
  We lay in positions love left us,
Watching a pane of light
  Slide over the moonlit furniture,

And then you would whisper
  All those place names in Europe,
Like a litany of ex-lovers
  Whom distance had made mythical.

I'd see dawn over Holland
  Where you laboured in a factory
And watched whitening skylights
  Mark another shift's completion.

Or endless rows of branches
  Stretching down Danish orchards,
Where three ribs were cracked
  In a strike of foreign pickers.

Sunday mornings in Hamburg,
  Down the steps at Jungfernstieg,
You feed bread from a booth
  To swans splashing on the river,

Or homesick some afternoon,
  You wander through the Reeperbahn,
Past neon striptease signs
  Where girls hustle in spitting rain.

Often I lose sight of you,
  Boarding a U-Bahn at Hauptbahnhof,
Shunted in a swaying tube
  To a migrant workers' hostel,

And mounting the third bunk
  In the stink of Turkish cigarettes
To re-imagine Dublin's streets
  Tattooed on veins on your wrist.

Or halted at a border post,
  Pulling a compartment window down
To watch the guard's flashlight
  Flicker on the wheels of the train,

Clutching your green passport
  In a limbo between foreign states,
Consumed with nostalgia
  For an identity irretrievably lost,

Which you tried to reclaim,
  Like the heir returned to an estate
Of hulks of gutted streets
  Being demolished for parking space,

Where bulldozers advanced,
  Flanked by a flotilla of children,
Swarming onto the safety frames
  In a grim carnival of destruction.

                    *

On your new motorbike
  In the April days after we met,
I would slip my hands
  Into the warmth of your jacket

And watch blurred tar
  Spin backwards beneath us,
As we rode past Ballymun
  Through a green maze of tunnels

Crazily paved with light,
  Shaken from overlapping branches,
That bordered the twisting roads
  Which swept onwards to Skerries.

I ignored the contradiction
  Between your vision and what I saw,
Because my pulse thrilled
  In the slipstream of your world.

But your world had died,
  Though you could not realise it:
A grey smudge of estates

Charted an encroaching horizon

Where apathetic children,
    Stared you down as we passed,
Like envoys from a rogue state
    Patrolled by stolen cars.

Gone were the fistfights
    And the flash of steel combs,
These blocks of flats sweated
    Under the reign of shotguns,

As you drew your legacy
    In a Victorian labour exchange
And saw every old friend
    Succumb to drugs or emigration.

                    *

Grief is a knot
    That is choking my throat,
Rage is a whirlwind
    Imploding through my skull.

If only I had known
    Your life to be in danger
I would have clawed
    My way between you and them.

I would have bitten
    Into their skin with my teeth,
I would have stubbed
    Out their eyes with my nails.

If only I had shouted
    When you walked from the flat,
Or ran to the balcony,
    Still naked, to call you back.

You went down steps
    Because the lift was broken,
You paused outside
    And strolled out of my life,

Across a courtyard
    Where women were talking,
Lying between sheets
    I heard your engine ignite.

I drifted into sleep
    To see a horse come riderless
Over fields trailing
    A bridle smeared with blood,

Towards a white house
    Where a woman stood screaming,
When I shuddered awake
    I realised her voice was mine.

I ran through side streets
    Where small clusters gathered
Whose eyes avoided mine
    When I raced frantically past,

Guided by their silence
    To the narrow tumbledown lane
In which singing blades
    Had ended their intimate work.

I knew they would get you
    Down some alleyway like this,
Ringed by silent gangs
    With both the exits blocked.

You never knew fear
    And that caused your death,
Trusting the familiar
    You roared into their trap.

You'd become an exile
    Stranded in your native city
Where the police distrusted,
    Your careful neutrality.

The drug dealers hated,
    Your naked contempt,
And youths growing up
    Coveted your motorbike

To be bartered in exchange
    For plastic bags of heroin,
They hovered, waiting,
    Every morning you left me.

One Friday a moneylender
    Arrived menacingly at our flat
Hunting an old neighbour.
    You grabbed his black folder,

Releasing the pages
    To scatter down into the yard,
Like fugitive particles
    From an exploding star

Which would eclipse us
   Within its blazing orbit.
I watched those pages
   Flutter into death warrants

That you simply ignored.
   In sleep I saw charred corpses
I could not recognise
   And hugged you till you woke,

Begging you to leave
   While we still might escape.
You smiled back at me,
   Listening to late-night traffic,

And said, in wonderment,
   Darling, I've finally come home,
Then curled up against me
   As if love could save us from harm.

                    *

My lament for you, Arthur Cleary,
   And for the life which we led,
For your laughter given freely
   From those blood-stained lips,

In that year we lived as one,
   Without priest or registrar
To bless the ringlets of sweat
   That tied our limbs together.

I will not put on black
   And spin out my life in mourning,
I will breathe your name

On the lips of another's children,

Like a secretive tongue
   They will carry in their hearts
To the foreign factories
   In which their lives will pass.

When loud sirens scream
   Across the European continent,
And they walk at dawn
   Towards scrubbed dormitories,

They will tell the fable
   Of the one who tried to return
And ride a glinting bike
   In a final gesture of freedom,

And envisage morning light
   Slanted down that crooked lane,
When their forefather fell
   And the new enslavement began.

Berlin/Dublin, 1985

From *Leinster Street Ghosts*
(1989)

The Buried Stream

There is a past
    You could not fathom
That remains present,
    That is waiting
For you to chance upon
    In your imagination.

    Young man,
These unsought words
    Are not yours.
Before your fathers came
    We dwelt here,
You did not invent us.

    Towards evening
We came forth to linger
    In this clearing
Beside the overhung river,
    With branches reflected
In fern-green trout pools
    Now piped underground.

We imagined your future:
    This apartment block
With its amber-lit car park
    Beneath which our bones rot,
And you at this table
    Hurriedly writing down
On this torn envelope
    Words not your own.

1986

Leinster Street Ghosts

In memory of Harry Sheridan

I

This was not supposed to be
    How our friendship ended:
Me leaning my head against
    My bare kitchen wall
To catch the murmuring
    Of curious mourners,
Packed into the smoky parlour
    Where you reluctantly sat
On days when it was too cold
    To haunt your front step.
You divided your life there
    Between music and talk shows,
Your ears always on the alert
    For any caller at our door.

Harry, you were supposed
    To miss me when I left,
Not leave me stranded,
    Aware of how you felt
At one a.m. on nights
    When poker hands were dealt
Across our kitchen table,
    And laughter echoed
With the clink of glasses
    To where you stood alone:
An eighty-year-old widower,
    Leaning on the adjoining wall

As you smiled, listening
    To friends who had gathered.

Behind you, the white dot
    On your ancient television
Reminded you that it was late
    And darkness beckoned
Up a stairs thronged with absence.
    How often had you hung your cap
Over the brass bedpost
    When you suddenly heard voices
Spilling out into the garden
    From our rented house next door?

You would curse yourself for giving up,
    When you might have appeared
From nowhere in your doorway –
    Like the ghost you have become –
To snatch one final chat
    From some sleepy gambler
Who would forever remember
    The wave, as he cycled home,
Of Harry Sheridan:
    A fierce man always to talk,
    A King amongst his words.

II

You hated harsh winters most
When you were trapped
    Like your tortoises asleep
In the cardboard box kept
    Beneath your kitchen press.
You sat alone with them,

Re-reading old newspapers,
Switching television channels,
    Always alert for the phone.

    You would be delighted
If ever I locked myself out,
    Coax me into your kitchen
And produce some old volume
    To keep the conversation going.
Next door, my unwritten novels
    Curled up at the edges.
I cursed you so often
    When kept late for a meeting
But now I cannot remember
    Those self-important faces;
What remains fresh in my mind
    Is carrying your shopping
Down to your smoky kitchen:
    The yellow-pack loaf of bread,
Parsnips and carrots mixed
    To be served with every meal.

    When squalls of snow fell
I walked the hushed streets,
    In pursuit of paraffin
To fill your ancient heater.
    You wore your hat indoors
To keep in all the heat,
    Smiling when I returned
With a new story on your lips.

'Have a drink,' you'd coax;
    A Nicotine-fingered teetotaller,
Uncorking a bottle of wine
    Opened twenty years before

To celebrate Mass said in Latin
  Among this same furniture.
Insects drowned in sediment
  In the glass I edged away,
Sitting on a wooden chair
  To hear your life story again.

Was there any Irish town
  Where you had never worked?
Any task of construction
  Your hands never undertook,
From tapping hammered gold-leaf
  On the Hospital Sweepstakes drum,
Or criss-crossing wartime Ireland
  Erecting Esso advertising hoardings,
To building Dublin's new estates
  As a journeyman carpenter,
While singing with the Palastrina Choir
  And the Dublin Grand Opera.

  Harry, I admired your guts:
Though on most days loneliness
  Ensnared you in its grip
You fought it every inch –
  No gambit too far-fetched
Not to be attempted.
  I'd know by the knock
You would be standing there
  With a 1910 Hotel Guide.
I would accept this new gift
  To file it away between
The pamphlet on John McCormack
  And Béaslái's *Life of Collins;*
Finally closing my front door
  With guilt and relief,

Visualising your return
      To your isolated kitchen
In the tortuous hour before dusk.

I will never be more welcome
      In any other place.

III

A birdhouse brightly painted
      When sons filled your rooms,
A mantelpiece of Wicklow stone
      Salvaged from a demolished house,
The photograph of a long-dead spaniel
      Who used to once bark there
Were the sole witnesses
      On the day you sat, slumped,
Your hand beside the fire
      Gradually growing burnt.
On the last day of autumn,
      Without telling a soul,
You cheated the winter.

I came down my stairs
      And heard your television
Blaring through the wall
      Without paying it any heed.
But I believe that you passed –
      A shadow on my ceiling –
To watch me one last time
      As I sat, self-absorbed,
Not knowing you were dead
      A dozen feet away from me,

In a kitchen where tortoises slept
    Boxed in the softest straw,
Who will wake again next spring
    And scratch at cardboard,
To shuffle forth, dazed from sleep,
    Bewildered by the luxury
Of thick carpet beneath their feet.

IV

I kept wanting to place
    One final loaf of bread
Among the floral wreaths
    That adorned your coffin.
I touched the polished wood
    And the brass handles,
Knowing you'd have admired
    Such fine craftsmanship.
When history selects heroes
    Men like you are excluded
But you are the only kind
    I still want to celebrate;

Workmen like you who shaped
    The streets where I was born
I will tell my future children
    How our Dublin history began
When an open-backed truck,
    Loaded down with furniture,
Was driven towards a Finglas estate
    Built by Harry Sheridan's hands.

1989

Owen

There are childhood jungles
        Of potato stalks,
Cropped ghosts of gardens
        That I have lost,
Where you belong
        Beside a rooted fork,
Weeding laden potato beds
        Until after dusk,
Coaxing a damp bonfire
        And breathing in
The reek of green leaves
        And sprinkled paraffin.

A dog barks under apple boughs,
        Rhode Island Reds scatter
As your hands seek the treasure
        Of eggs hidden in straw.
A kitchen door is framed in light
        As the evening dissolves
In a chorus of rural accents.
        The scent of baking wafts
From your hard-won *lebensraum*
        To this floodlit balcony
Where I wait for news of you,
        My favourite uncle.

How you would love this night:
        A cold nocturnal breeze,
The creaking limbs of sycamore
        Softened by amber light.
I start a cigarette for you,
        Inhale as slowly as I can,

When its tip has burnt out
        Your life will have gone.
For now you are corralled
        Between hospital sheets,
Hands plucking at blankets,
        Weakly trying to rise.

'I'm dying and I don't want to.'
        Who can reply to such words,
Beyond to hope that a garden exists
        Where leaves are never burnt
Like the lining on your lung
        After radiation treatment.
Perhaps all that awaits is emptiness.
        I just know that one hour ago
Your drugged eyes burnt open
        With a saturating blueness
As you whispered names of sisters
        Who are long in the grave.

Soon it will be spring again
        In the gardens of Finglas,
Lilac and cherry blossom
        Will bloom in your absence.
Another child will run
        Home from the chip shop,
Moist beads of vinegar
        Staining his jacket,
His thoughts already turned
        Towards a future abroad,
Away from this suburban terrace
        Your countryman's hands bought

With weekly money orders sent
        From an English car plant.

Rhubarb and cabbage sown
     Before re-boarding the boat,
In expectation of a better time
     When you could finally return.
How could you have known
     Mass emigration would start again.
Fewer of your neighbours will lean
     Over garden walls this spring,
Fewer drinkers will companionably argue
     Across Martins' pub table,

Fewer new families will be left
     To plant shrubs in your place
Whorls of lilac will wither
     Unplucked on the branch.
Above me a late-night jet
     Winks one bloodshot eye,
Transporting an aisle of young faces
     In an updated newsreel.

I try to shield the hot filter,
     But the cigarette is finished,
Glow-worms of ash scatter
     Down towards the car park.
The telephone is ringing,
     I step through the door:
It takes me a lifetime
     To lift the receiver.

1986

A Memory of Madeleine Stuart

Down two potholed furlongs of tarmac
      She watched the postman descend,
Already aware by the bulge in his bag
      That the manuscript had been returned.

After she placed it on the kitchen table
      She walked out into the garden
Where Francis knelt among rows of plants,
      Sensing, by the pause of his hands,
That he knew without her needing to speak.

Until darkness stole away their shape
      She maintained her vigil by his side
Watching his arthritic fingers nurse the soil,
      Coaxing tall ungainly sunflowers
To miracously lift their florets in autumn light.

1986

Beechwood Avenue

I want it back:
Your floorboards where I slept
    In a blissful stupor,
Not bothering to get undressed.
    I want to wake,
Wrecked beneath a blanket;
    The aftertaste
Of whiskey scorching my throat,
    With my limbs –
Immersed in the magnified light
    Drenching through
Those high latticed panes of glass –
    Being stiffly revived
By hungover, exhausted happiness.

I want the hunger
Of anticipation inside night clubs,
    Our elation mirrored
In a waitress's eyes dilated by Seconal.
    I want to shuffle
For Seven Card and Five Card Stud
    While a water pipe
Gets passed among a circle of gamblers.
    I want to squander
Every penny kept for the taxi fare,
    And be forced to walk
Past dawn-lit prostitutes on the canal
    Back to your flat
To toss pebbles against your window.

I want to make love
Carelessly again in a slanted attic
        With a bay window besieged
By a swaying fantasia of branches,
        While myriad parties erupt
Like a trail of discarded fireworks
        From behind each flat door
Inside that labyrinth of plywood bedsits.
        I want to plunder
A girl's black bicycle from the hallway,
        To career straight into
A tree trunk growing on the pavement,
        And leave brain cells
Strewn like mementoes across the city.

        Then, when it is over,
I want to wake again in Beechwood,
        On the same floorboards
Between your bed and wardrobe;
        And open my eyes,
Hypnotized by immaculate virgin light:
        My soul as pure as a child
Trapped in a dark confession box
        When the slit slides open
And the mesh of light cascades
        Onto his celibate face
And his devoutly raised eyes,
        With his throat ablaze
From a hunger he will never satisfy.

1987

Wishbone

Do not be afraid, my oldest friend,
  To send a sign that you are gone:
    In the malaise after your funeral

   Visit me unexpectedly some morning:
  Your face behind mine in the mirror,
Glimpsed for an instant, startlingly young.

1988

Leinster Street

For Bernie

I

Let us wake in Leinster Street,
      Both of us still twenty-six,
On a spring Monday in 1985.
      We lie on, relaxed, illicit,
Listening to the chatter below
      Of friends cooking breakfast.

Flaking paint on the lattice,
      Old wire, crumbling stone:
The silos of the abandoned mill
      Framed by windows which open
Onto flowers that are lodged
      Between bricks in the lane.

And no need for us to rise
      For another drowsy hour:
Lie on with me in that moment
      When you were still too shy
To dress yourself while I watched
      Your limbs garbed in light.

II

In those rooms five years passed
      In a single drawn-out breath
Before we all plunged into new lives.
      Remember how the ceiling wept
Beneath each rafter in the winter,
      The rustle of shuffled cards that crept

Up unlit stairways after midnight.
      May some tenant of the future
Turn when switching out their light
      And, framed by the doorway, glimpse
The phosphorescence of our lives
      Still glowing with this happiness.

1989

From *Taking My Letters Back* (1998)

Prayer

I have come this long journey without finding you
        Or casting off your reflection;

Have tried a dozen obsessions without cleansing
        Your taste from my tongue.

Oldest friend and adversary; fugitive brother,
        We recognise each other

In carriages of express trains that pass:
        Your hands beat on the glass.

1997

Wherever You Woke

There only ever was one street,
    One back garden, one bedroom:
Wherever you woke, you woke beneath

    The ceiling where you were born,
For the briefest unconscious second
    An eyelid's flutter from home.

1994

Lines for an Unknown Uncle

In memory of Francis Bolger, Green Street, Wexford, died 3 June 1928

No son or granddaughter to remember you:
    No trace of your seventeen years left,
Except in the mind of your younger brother

    Sent out onto the street to wait,
While you screamed in the height of fever
    For someone to finish you with an axe.

1998

April Bright

New owners have refurbished these rooms
   During the five decades since her death,
      Yet occasionally when sunlight floods in

April's sixteen-year-old ghost races unseen
   Though the bricked-up partition wall
      Where her bedroom door had been.

Breathlessly descends each stair,
   In a saturating blaze of evening light,
      She flicking back bobbing hair

From her carefree, radiant features,
   While joyously running towards the open
      Arms of her truncated future,

With her blue eyes so alert
   And sleek limbs as virginal
      As the cotton handkerchief

In the breast pocket
   Of her school uniform –
      Which she could not don

To veil her brunette curls
   When she wished to light
      A candle in the chapel,

Because its clean white fibres
   Were stained with clotted blood
      She had suddenly coughed up.

1991

Poem Found in a Faded Newspaper

I

Imagine this poem, boxed
   Among columns of newsprint,
      In the evening paper you half-read

On the night when you move
   Into the first house you own.
      How eerie these rooms seem

Beneath bare light bulbs:
   Strips of unfaded carpet
      Like sunken graves marking

Where furniture once stood.
   You have stacked paint tins
      Beside the solitary mattress.

Tomorrow new carpets will arrive.
   You finger the thin-bladed knife,
      Already hearing in your mind

The trundle of a child's tricycle,
   Bare feet, muffled by underlay,
      Racing to greet your return home.

It is midnight before you start.
   This poem becomes the sole witness
      To how you rip up the old carpets

To make these rooms feel your own.
   The floorboards naked for you to possess,
      Yet all you can do is lay newspaper down.

II

Decades pass and you will be dead
When a new owner lifts these carpets.

Your house stripped bare as they glance
At this poem; trying to somehow fathom

Your unknowable life, your thoughts tonight,
Through these faded lines you only half-read.

1993

Algae Hibernicae

A collection of seaweed specimens assembled by William McCalla,
1814–1849

Your fingers press down samples of seaweeds
In Roundstone, Connemara, in the spring of 1845,
With no portents yet of how neighbours will die.

You cross the rocks, a schoolmaster's ambitious son,
Transcribing into Latin from your Gaelic tongue
The species of each alga that you can identify.

In the Botanic Gardens, where your work will reside,
David Moore bends among flowering beds to spot
A fungal blight blemishing rows of potato stalks.

Soon cholera will plunder your last breath.
Neighbours will disperse like sycamore sepals
Into open pits, coffin ships and workhouses;

Or slave on grand follies that will never match
The Curvilinear Range Glasshouse rising above
The belly of Dublin city, swollen with hunger,

Where famished beggars outside the Botanic Gardens
Will watch sumptuous glass panes slotted into place
To shelter exotic plants stolen from tropical slopes.

And in the herbarium there a space will be found
For the seaweeds you now press with such hopes
Of advancement into your collection, *Algae Hibernicae,*

While barefoot children swarm about on the rocks
Where flies will soon buzz around their bloated lips,
Green from eating seaweed and half-digested grass.

1994

Polygonum Baldschuanicum

Colloquial names: 'Russian Vine' or 'Mile-a-Minute'

One day it shall be you who will inherit
      Every house and shed and crevice
Leading to every penthouse, lift-shaft or billet.

Rooftops of tangled blossoms entwining,
      Tendrils glistening in rooms
That light and voices have long forsaken.

No place will have escaped your noose
      Of leaves and shoots; a green python
Choking our civilization: this dozing goose,
      Who forgot to sleep with one eye open.

1994

Ireland, 1967

For Aengus Fanning

Nothing much happened around here back then:
The young became an array of foreign stamps
Illuminating the mantelpieces of ageing parents
Waiting for crops, death or drainage grants.

But occasionally old men would crane their necks
At the distant drone of a solitary helicopter
That soared against the sun: a glinting speck

Of hope that sods might soon be turned, bricks laid
By Brylcreamed Young Turks stepping from Mercs
To conjure fairy-dust factories and sink mine-shafts.

The future flew beyond them, immeasurably perfect:
They could imagine his mohair suit and handclasp,
As they gazed, gape-mouthed, convincing themselves
That the minister himself had swept majestically past.

1995

Taking My Letters Back

For Sheila Fitzgerald

The envelope rests like a coffin
  In my glove compartment.
I have parked at this turning
  By the old schoolhouse
Where local artists cheerfully work
  In batik, oils and poverty.

Beyond an acre of stacked rafters
  Salvaged from a closed asylum,
Past a honeycomb of tyre tracks
  I glimpse the mobile home
Where you happily live at ninety-one,
  Among the exuberant young.

I am taking back my early letters
  In case they get burnt
In the bonfire after your death.
  When I re-read them last night,
It did not seem to be your spirit
  That was in danger of extinction,

Besieged by all this activity,
  But the soul of the teenage boy
Who typed poems on carbon paper,
  Unable to afford a new ribbon,
And hitched across Ireland to read them
  Aloud in your candlelit caravan.

When I finally learn that you are gone
  I will recall driving off at dawn
In this same steadfast silence
  In which you once carried home,
To your wild woodland lawn,
  The ashes of your son.

Kilmore, Wexford, 1994

'Last Songs' by Francis Ledwidge

I hold this volume you have never seen,
Published by Herbert Jenkins of London
During the Armistice of nineteen eighteen,

After whatever of your limbs they could salvage
Were re-buried in grave number 5, row B,
The Second Plot, Artillery Wood Cemetery.

When I was younger you felt like a brother,
At night I longed for your ghost to haunt me.

Now, reading these poems again, what I reject
Are the flaws that I abhor in my younger self.

We essentially have little in common, Frank,
Yet I know that when it comes my turn
To venture down the tunnel of the unknown

You will be among the hallucinogenic ranks
Of shuffled faces conjured up in welcome.
Finally we shall recognise each other.

1996

Going Home for Christmas

For Betty

Mohill and Abbeyfeale, Kinvara and Rathvilly
Were the home towns of girls for whom my feelings
Went silently unrequited in the branch libraries.

I'd requisition road atlases – shelved at 912.415 –
And trace their weekly homecoming by private bus
To Louisburgh and Ferns, remote realms of Offaly.

Each girl's place-name in turn so captivated me
That now, passing road signs for them in December,
I cannot see narrow streets of small shop windows,

Advertising local bands and Christmas Club Specials.
It's the effervescent features of young girls I see,
With strands of tumble-weed hair illuminating

The roadway, sweeping back, twisting around corners
To light up damp alleyways and bustling main streets
Where buses from the past stop for them to alight

Into the arms of loved ones and lovers at Christmas:
In Mohill and Abbeyfeale, Kinvara and Rathvilly:
Ghosts from the 1980s, in their first flame of beauty.

1997

Martha

I found the box of old albums,
Blew dust off a disused needle,

Tom Waits began to sing 'Martha'.
Once again I was twenty-four,

The pull of hash and tobacco,
Cheap white wine at my elbow

At the window of your bedsit
In the dust-filled August light.

A needle bobbing over warped vinyl
One final time before we stroll

Down to bars where friends gather.
Decks to be shuffled, numbers rolled,

Blankets bagged on some dawn-lit floor.
Our lives are just waiting to occur

As we linger in the infinity that it takes
For the voice of Tom Waits to fade.

1995

In Memory of Rory Gallagher

1948–1995

There came a time on teenage summer nights
    When a free house had been found,
And a cheap stereo rigged with strobe lights
    That froze each moment in your mind.

You just knew when the crowd had waned
    And the wasters had long gone
That soon the clued-in boys who remained
    Would put Rory Gallagher on.

16 June 1995

Temple Street Children's Hospital

This is your territory, I brought you here:
Shoddy tenement windows where washing flaps,
Crumbling lanes where cars get broken for parts.

There is an archway beneath which we passed –
Like the one above which you shared a flat
With your sisters up from Monaghan for work

In a war-becalmed Dublin. Surely you must once
Have gazed up, puzzled by how the years since
Had landed you here with a son, a stuttering misfit,

Unable to pronounce the most simple of words;
A bright penny whose cloud you'd never see lift
As you fretted, unaware of how close death hovered.

The speech therapist's office had fancy toys and books
And a special mirror which allowed me to be watched.
The waiting room contained a white merciless clock

That ticked off the final hours we spent alone,
Gazing down at a garden where I yearned to walk;
Trapped indoors by the shame of my garbled tongue.

*

I stand outside that hospital in Nerney's Court,
At Kelly's Row where a blacksmith once worked,

And no logic can explain why you feel this close,
Why I see us in the mother and child who pass,

Or how, as I age, I slowly become your son,
Gazing through your eyes with incomprehension.

I was too young to have known you, so it makes no sense
That every passing year only deepens your absence.

1996

Ash Wednesday

For Brian Keenan

From a distance the entire city
  Wears a bullet hole in its forehead,
Except for the track-suited children,
  Racing beneath the builders' cranes,
With plastic pistols in their hands.

The Lenten box squats on shop counters,
  Emblazoned with a starving child
Staring into the aimed photo lens
  As though the click of the shutter
Would blow his shaved head asunder.

The world's mental age is twelve.
  It has nothing left to give up.
Children inside the limbs of men
  Swarm out, screaming about God,
And masturbate with their guns.

Ash Wednesday, 1993

Millbourne Avenue, Winter

Three-quarter moon and a scatter of stars,
A frost that is not yet hard,
A dog's clear bark, a chemist's sign
Flashing cold blue light, on and off.

A cat crouching above the old man's shop
Who sold knick-knacks and colouring books,
And the warmth pulsing through my legs
That have left the bed where we made love.

1993

Holotropic Botanicus

I close my eyes to find before me
　　A wooden door with a silver handle,
　　　　Which I feel unable to open,
　　　　　　That opens by itself, inwardly.

Beyond it, a nightscape of stars
　　Weakens down to the glimmer
　　　　Of a sweating pane of glass,
　　　　　　Curved within corroding girders.

The Waterlily House of the Botanic Gardens;
　　My son's face moistened in the sultry light,
　　　　We are seated by the plopping waterwheel
　　　　　　And we are smiling across at each other.

I only realise when the vision is dissipating
　　That I am him and the tall figure my mother:
　　　　Goldfish flit through the green water
　　　　　　And we are smiling across at each other.

1993

On a Train in England

For Dylan Michael Gwyn Jones

You will never know of this moment:
The Northern landscape of England passing
As this stranger pauses, slightly reticent
To ask your mother if she wishes for children.

I cannot tell if her smile belies hope or regret,
Our train surges on, cities pass.
Her hands are folded, feeling for each secret
Flutter of your feet close to her heart.

1998

Three Seasons For My Sons

Walking on a Spring Evening with My Two Sons

Let us search for tractors and motorbikes.
Let the evening remain bewitched in promise;
With the man who locks the gates of the park
A distant sandman still not impeding our horizon.

And let me see the world made fresh in your eyes
As we look for birds nesting in sycamore and ash;
Let both your right hands nestle in my palms
As you point, wonder-struck, at trailers and trucks,

And we stride with such tremendous purpose
After our long shadows that stretch along the path.

Griffith Park, Drumcondra, 1994

Collecting Chestnuts with My Sons, September, 1995

These lines are written because I cannot tell
What permutations for us all may lie ahead.
Therefore I wish to record for you the fact
That we collected – in the space of an hour

And within one hundred yards of our house –
Three hundred and ninety one fallen chestnuts;
Many still cocooned in thick, prickly shells,
The others glinting amid the drenched grass.

When another three decades have passed
Will children still hunt here for chestnuts?
Shall these boughs have long been felled

By freak storm, melt-down or pestilence,
Or will thirty new rings encircle their hearts
As excited children crack shells on the path?

There is so little we can honestly predict,
Except that children inevitably look back
At the modernity parents felt we lived in

To see how life was backward and simpler then.
So much of your lives will have already occurred,
Such roots set down across an altered world,

That these lines may be all you have to recall
This ordinary Sunday, after a night of squalls,

As you raced beneath leaves still dripping wet
To cram every pocket of your father's jacket

With the polished whorls of smooth chestnuts;
My two beautiful sons, aged three and aged five,
Scampering off again to plunder the opened husks
That waited to be spied by your flawless eyes.

24 September 1995

The Constellations of Drumcondra

Who knows what records you may break
 Or what goals the world will set you,
But there is no voyage you'll undertake
 With a purpose so clear and absolute
As this search in the December twilight
 For the sparkle of lit trees in windows.

How many shall I count, walking tonight,
 Wrapped up for the cold with my boys?
Breaking our record of two hundred and six
 Leaves neither of you satisfied,
Knowing there must be one last cul-de-sac
 Whose array has not yet been spied.

Cities won't always have seasons like this:
 Chestnuts like manna in the autumn grass,
Blackberries growing wild in the colleges,
 And candles in windows in the wintry dark.
You will grow older, losing your innocence,
 And, with luck, eventually gaining it back.

But may you never lose the sense of resolve
 With which you both grip my hand
Beneath a skyline of stars foretelling frost,
 And lead me around a penultimate bend
Onto a street alive with leaping sword-fish
 And acrobats from the fantastical land

Which spills over from your imaginations.
 There, amid the constellations of Drumcondra,

You eventually reach the magical number
   That, by unspoken consent, allows us to turn,
Astronomers, explorers returning from afar
   To glimpse the final lit window that is home.

December 1996

From *The Chosen Moment*
(2004)

The Chosen Moment

For Bernie

The second that it took for three sailors to sip
The dregs of a war-time round of stout
Made him miss the last bus back to his ship:
Made my father change vessels, meet a girl, slip
Into the orbit of love that brought me about.

That moment two bicycles slowed to a halt
Outside Trinity College on a January night:
Our future spun like a coin as we thought
To separate after two dates, keeping everything light,
Unaware we each were what the other sought.

Lives are woven together by intricate layers
Of chance and circumstance: by snap decisions
When love unexpectedly, inexplicably beckons
Through doors opening out into all these years,
Hinged onto such slim unbeknownst seconds.

The Brigadier

In memory of Francis Stuart, 1902–2000

Dawn. A steep hill into a shadow-strewn glen
Where the Military Road falls, unearthly straight.
Cradling a white cat, the tall angular man
Descends with his slow, contemplative's gait.

Waiting by the bridge, a brigadier, equally old:
Both veterans of all that there is to be seen.
Neither speaks while the long silence unfolds,
Their features gravely inquisitorial yet serene.

'Report, corporal,' the brigadier says at length.
'I loved. I made for some small creatures an ark.'
'Is that all? Nothing else to cite in your defence?'
Silence. The flicker of a smile. 'You may pass.'

Drumcondra Bridge

Three lanes become two here, motorists joust
In their daily game to see who will blink first.

Every afternoon when I approach this bridge
I relive the second when the cyclist strayed

To avoid a pothole that blocked her passage;
Her glimpse of water through the balustrade

As a car brushed the college books on her carrier
With the faintest touch so she swerved and fell.

Traffic crept past while passers-by encircled her,
Motionless and hushed as if bound by a spell.

Her back wheel still spun when it had fallen,
With her face hidden, no hint of hair or clothes,

But peeping out from an oil-streaked tarpaulin
Two breathtakingly white slender bare soles.

A Poet of the 1950s

Out of print and out of mind since your death,
Yet your rapt lyrics still reside like fugitives
Inside shrewd anthologies of modern Irish verse.

Vessels for your love, fragility and indignation,
Crafted in decreasing circles while you flitted
From boardroom to hunt ball to discreet asylum.

In the local golf club a few older men still recall
Your sports car and dancing with your daughter.
They never heard you wrote poems or of any fame:

They only ever heard the retort of the single gunshot
And found your body lying against the door-frame.

At Twenty

She said, '*I'm suffering from a terrible flu,*
If we sleep together I'll pass it on to you.'

He lay in bed for four days after she left,
Shivering and waking up drenched in sweat,
His throat raw, legs unable to take his weight:
He paid this price happily, with no regret.

A Steep Lane in Monaghan

In memory of Patrick Flanagan

Who can measure the journey undergone,
From being carried up this steep lane by your father

After baptism to his remote hillside farm,
To being carried from the same farmhouse by your sons

Out into the darkness of a gale-force storm,
To be borne down the same lane on their shoulders,

Past neighbours with astute appreciation
Of eight decades spent traversing eight hundred yards.

November 2002

Remembering Certain Golf Holes

For Roger

Most are forgotten before you reach the next tee.
Encounters, not as brief as they might have been:
A mixed-bag of drives, chips and scrambled bogeys.

But certain holes resurface in your mind at night:
That stillness at the pitch of a perfect swing,
Rushes and swamp, trees split by shafting light

As pussy willow billows wild in some ditch.
The instant when a white ball soared or rolled
And life elsewhere momentarily ceased to exist.

Often you lie awake, longing to replay some shot
With what semblance of sense you've since picked up.
But you would happily repeat every single mistake

For the moment your shot carried the lake and furze
Onto a fairway curving past trees placed to punish
Any golfer who avoids taking on the nest of bunkers.

You watched your ball rise, like a starling taking fright,
To get lost against the blueness of an evening skyline,
Where you were lost too, bewitched by the arc of its flight.

Absent Friends

For Deirdre

Dusk on Christmas Eve, a dozen tasks to be done.
The bustle of excited children playing downstairs,
Shopping that must be unpacked, decorations hung.

Amidst this bustle I sometimes find myself alone
In my bedroom, forgetting what I came up to fetch,
As I am swamped by a mosaic of faces once known.

Soon I will go down to celebrate with my loved ones,
But I need to honour the presences who shaped me first.
I open my bedroom window to let absent friends come.

Approaching My 45th Birthday

For Paddy Farrell

The younger men fall off on nights like this.
Initially nobody appears in the teeming hailstones
Where floodlights illuminate a deserted pitch.

Then from nowhere a handful of cars emerge.
The drivers stare out at the February gale
And exchange glances through their windows.

Surely nobody with any sanity would play soccer
In this monsoon when not even a dog would stir,
But then one door opens and slagging voices call

To ageing men with bad backs and strapped ankles,
Who clamber out to limber up, laughing at the downpour,
Knowing we won't be blessed by such Fridays forever.

Let There Be Space

For Kazem Sharahari

Let there be space for an apricot tree to grow:
Once such a space exists it can become a home.
Each night in your Parisian courtyard you go

To touch its soft fruit and survey the firmament
That framed these same constellations over Persia
In a childhood with no thoughts of imprisonment,

Police beatings and your torturous trek into exile.
Your children dream in French, walk to school
Amid immigrant tongues, in an arrondissement

Of steep cobbled streets and paint-flaked apartments.
But behind your small gate this garden exists,
A miracle of space where one can write and think

In Persian and French and in no known tongue:
Just an empty lexicon which can only be filled
By the voices of your children who call it home.

Strangers

In memory of Bridie Bolger & Mary Clifton

In Baggot Street during the war their paths surely cross:
Two young women from farms in Monaghan and Cavan
Commencing new lives in Dublin as a waitress and a nurse.

Possibly they register their similarities with a glance
Before being swept back into their separate worlds.
They never knew one another and never got the chance

To hold the two grandsons they share in common.
Both women died far too young, consumed by cancer
And by concerns for sons and daughters left behind.

I can only light two white candles side by side for them,
At the shrine of *St Thérèse de l'Enfant Jésus*,
Here in the hushed cathedral of Our Lady of Reims.

After The Chase

In memory of Linda Mullally, 1978–2002

After the chase through years of watching eyes,
With every warren blocked, every gate closed over,
The world a jerky blur, spinning out of focus,
Terrified of bony fingers seizing your shoulder:

For the first time in a decade you pause to breathe
With no fat witch pursuing you, no mocking echo,
Just the sound of your heart allowing itself to rest
And the peace of a pulse that grows eternally slow.

The chasing hounds are left behind in the forest
Where sharp branches snagged your hair and skirt,
Trying to flee the spell you become entrapped in,
Where down every corridor a trick mirror lurked.

Beyond the forest edge, whether mirage or real,
Lies an ocean, so clear and tantalisingly blue,
That its waters restore a time when you were happy,
They restore to you a time when you were you.

Whales are calling from the depths of clear water,
Amid dolphin-song, in tones you've always known,
You swim above loved ones watching over your bed
Towards the watchers over them who summon you home.

27 May 2002

Letters Sent Back in 19th Century Copies of *The Annals for Propagation of the Faith*, Abandoned in the Attics of All Hallows Seminary

Perhaps all printed words eventually share our fate.
Stacked here among bric-a-brac, obsolete maps
And photographs of dead men with no descendants.

Workmen have punched holes in the brickwork
To overhaul Victorian plumbing, exposing innards
Of pipes and flaking plaster in their search for dry rot.

Undisturbed amid this rubble, we reside beside crates
Of *Duffy's Weekly Volume of Catholic Divinity*,
Here in *The Annals for Propagation of the Faith*.

Long-robed correspondents shaped us into sentences:
Fishermen of a vanished empire, servants of certitude
Who cast luminous nets over desert and rainforest.

They entreat readers to pray while recording their catch:
How a woman hid baptismal water beneath her cloak
To snatch the pagan soul of a dying child for Christ.

We were salmon, somehow finding our route home
From the open sewers of diseased shantytowns
To these seminary corridors where we were spawned

Amid silent prayer in bare cells lit by a tallow dip,
During solitary games of handball in the sleety rain
And rapt nights kneeling on stone floors in worship.

Corralled here by full stops, anchored to each page,
We cannot betray if with their final rasping breath
Our authors saw Christ stride or sink amid the waves.

We are logbooks of floundered ships, yellow with age,
Marooned on dusty shelves beneath high arched rafters,
In the belly of a beached whale with a wooden ribcage.

The Baily Lighthouse

For Bill Long

Some nights I dream I am back in that watch room,
Assailed by the salt-spray of waves on every side;
Oblivious to how the optic lens high in the lanthorn
Casts its beam, measured at a million candelas bright,
Positioned forty metres above the mean spring tide,
So that each fourteen seconds of darkness is punctured
By one solitary flash that illuminates the sea with light.

During every flash the indentured part of me is exposed,
Still bent there at a desk, typing with slow finger strokes
Over the incessant crackle from the short-wave radio.
That part of me which real life could never quite reclaim,
Engrossed in some novel, with my back to the window,
Alone with phantoms who continually haunt my brain,
Unheeded by seabirds and seals basking on the rocks below.

The Former Lady Golf Captain

For the late Jim Donoghue

Something about how the slant of sunlight
Penetrates this maze of hawthorn and briars
To cast a swaying mosaic of shadows
On the muddy path to the tee-markers,
Always ambushes her with the memory
Of light flickering over the unblinking eyes
Of a dead boy who gazed up, as if amazed
By the periwinkle-blue of the Kerry sky.

No other soul was present that morning,
Just her twenty-year-old self and this youth
Who had casually leapt out from a clearing
In the certitude that cars never strayed
Up the unapproved mountainous route
Which she had driven onto by mistake,
So absorbed in studying her touring map
That she had precious time to brake.

That accident occurred a half century ago,
Yet an imprint of the trauma endured
Still lurks here to stealthily ensnare her
Sometimes when passing this hedgerow;
The sadness with which she never burdened
The husband whom she nursed to his death,
Unaware of how she bore a dark pearl of grief
Since that speck of grit lodged in her heart.

She has glimpsed the boy's bemused stare
Within the eyes of her young granddaughter,

And still spots him on bustling escalators
As his doppelgänger continues to haunt her
Through the five decades without absolution
When she trained her mind to forget him
By reinventing herself as a formidable figure:
A retired school principle, a former lady captain.

But sometimes during the Tuesday foursomes,
When the spring sunlight slants like this,
The shadows swaying on the muddy path
Still cause her to pause to catch her breath
And relive the loneliness in which she knelt
To cradle this boy as tenderly as any first born,
Beneath a periwinkle-blue Kerry skyline
In an unpaved lane besieged by hawthorn.

Her golfing partners cease to gossip beside her,
As they reach the first tee on the closing nine.
Bracing herself against this phantom pain,
She crafts a measured five-wood into the wind.

Verses Put Aside Between
My 40th and 41st Birthday

So much time wasted in so many rooms.
        I am exactly half my father's age.
His sea voyages have ended, the swell
        Of waves causing his cabin to roll
In a cargo vessel of containers tossed about
        On storm-lashed shipping lanes.
He has time now for whiskey in an armchair,
        Visiting each child's home in turn,
Savouring retirement like a savvy King Lear.

My sons play at being chefs as I type this poem,
        Cooking illusory pizzas under a bed:
Their excited chatter fills our terraced home.

There are so many other rooms where I have sat.
        So many hideaways I could enumerate:
Listing books and plays completed, draft by draft,
        As is they might explain the vanished decades
I reflect on. Can that really be me at twenty-one,
        Sprawled on a table in a courthouse canteen,
Eavesdropping on criminals out in the corridor
        Before the duty guard announces their case?
I feel trapped in this library job where time
        Needs to be speeded up during the office hours
I spend seeking books stored on the court balcony
        While below me judges impersonate Mr Punch.

But I've skipped ahead too fast. I must flit back
        Past trays of welding rods in the factory

Where I hang out with Eugene, chewing raw hash
        While each night shift inches past
As torturously ponderous as an ancient tortoise,
        As we wait for skylights to brighten.

I am awaiting the bell in a Finglas classroom;
        Waiting to celebrate my twelfth birthday;
Retreating to the bedrock of my first memory
        Of happily playing with clothes pegs
As my singing mother hangs washing in our garden.

Look: here I am at seven, unless I misremember,
        In the boxroom with its ventilation hole
Through which I'm terrified ghosts will enter.
        I close my eyes; pull bedclothes tighter,
Terrified that monsters may lurk overhead.
        Why am I so scared? What can I recall
About nightmares of snakes slithering across lino?
        Crying in the dark that I have no friends,
Curling up beneath the blankets like an embryo.

I roll up four socks to create a ball and throw it:
        It bounces off the bedroom wall
For me to volley home another winner for Ireland.
        Children play outside on the road.
My mother has died. I am alone in that house,
        Keeping pain at bay by tossing a ball
At the wall to score spectacular imaginary goals.

I patrol empty rooms: the ten-year-old curator
        Of the home in which I was born
After a midwife untangled a cord I was choking on.
        Every room radiates its separate fear,

The pig's face glimpsed at an upstairs window,
        The ghostly figure haunting the stairs.

I lock the bathroom door, imagining whispers
        From the attic or the closed wardrobe
Where I hung my father's black mourning tie.
        Alone at night, I conjure my first poems
On the huge typewriter my brother procured,
        Drowning the silence with clamorous keys.

The rooms I live in grow as untidy as my plans.
        My father still at sea, my siblings married.
When I can't afford to purchase a typewriter ribbon
        I type unseen poems onto carbon paper.
At nineteen I find factory work. Returning at dawn
        I put a blanket on the window to stifle daylight,
Then wake and resume typing until my shift starts.

Fast-forward a decade: our first child is being born:
        I frantically seek a taxi on frozen roads.
When we take him home and peer into his carrycot,
        As if he was a time-bomb about to explode,
I try to imagine my son and I being forty and ten.
        They seem impossible ages back then,
As I wheel him in the park or let him down to crawl,
        Longing for the day when he learns to walk
Like the toddler under the trees kicking football.

Yet, miraculously, here we are, aged forty and ten.
        Time has pushed on with bewildering pace
To the threshold of the Twenty-First Millennium,
        To a new century that will belong to my sons.
What can I tell them about mine? What can I pass on
        When all I have learnt is how little I know?

At the end of my century that ceased to make sense
       My only wish is to hold their growing hands
And marvel at the magnitude of my ignorance.

And at this miracle I could never have envisaged
       As a youth walking Finglas streets
Each night, pacing out verse metres in my mind
       As a poultice against loneliness –
That I'd be blessed to find somebody to share my life,
       To watch over me, recognising how I move
Between real and fictional worlds, needing my daily ration
       Of three meals, a thousand words and love.

My sons' imaginary pizzas are nearly cooked.
       Soon I will ask permission to kneel
And be allowed to share in their make-believe.
       Their guileless eyes and incomparable gift
For absolute absorption in each game they play,
       Reminds me how last night I dreamt that I stood
In my father's overgrown garden, reunited with the girl
       Who once helped me to plant a chestnut sprig
That an elderly Protestant neighbour gave to us.
       In my dream this tree blocks out the skyline
As we stand beneath it now, three decades on,
       Staring up at its maze of thick branches
That reflect the journeys our lives have undergone.

Although we both know how time has passed,
       The girl in my dream has not changed.
As I gaze at Zeta's immaculate nine-year-old face
       I felt simultaneously a child and a man.
In adolescence we lost touch with one another,
       Venturing into divergent adult worlds,
But my dream throws us back together
       Into that marvellous ease of childhood.

We feel no need to exchange a single word.
         We just gaze up at this tree we planted
And as I peer into its immense greenness,
         I experience an inexplicable consolation
At knowing how this tree still soars into the sky,
         With each new ring of gleaming bark
Marking another year in these onwards voyages
         Towards destinations we will eventually discern.

But, defying time, my memories remain strong
         Of that day in vibrant sunlight as we run,
Carrying a sprig from an old neighbours's garden
         Across the heart-stopping world of the young.

From *External Affairs*
(2008)

Ballymun Incantation

Whose voice can you hear?
>Who's that calling down the stair?

What ghost trapped in a lift shaft?
>What child who played and laughed?

In nineteen hundred and sixty-seven,
>Craning our necks towards heaven,

We arrived here by truck and bus,
>Three thousand families of us.

Tea chests and cardboard suitcases,
>Boxes bound with old shoelaces,

From tenements in condemned streets,
>Now the world appeared at our feet;

Crowding the lifts and up each stair,
>Onto the balconies to breathe the air,

We were so dizzy all Dublin spun:
>The chosen families of Ballymun.

I think this heat is killing us.
>Why can't we turn off the radiators?

Where are the shops we were promised?
>Why won't they come to fix the broken lifts?

My name is Mary, when I turned nine
>I slept alone for the first time,

My sister whispering secrets overhead
>In Ceannt Tower in a new bunk bed.

In Plunkett Tower my wife grew shook,
>She was alone when the lift got stuck,

She hated the squatters jarring her nerves,
 I still see her shaking, reciting prayers.

My name is Agnes, when I was born,
 The Civil War was still raging on.
I moved to Balcurris with my grandchildren,
 I lived for Novenas and for Sweet Afton.

My name is John, I stole my first kiss
 Just before the doors opened in the lift,
Eilish was still in her school uniform;
 I believed no other love could be so strong.

Help me, I'm still lost here and all alone,
 I injected my mother's hopes into my arm,
Shivering in the depths of cold turkey
 I thought I could fly from this balcony.

Why won't the voices stop whispering,
 Straining to be heard amid the babbling?
Lives that were ended and lives begun;
 The living and the dead of Ballymun.

Remember my name, it is Elizabeth,
 In the local workhouse I faced my death.
Cholera stole away my famished son,
 I buried him amid the fields of Ballymun.

Remember me; my ghost also haunts here,
 Seeking my child who fell through the air.
The coroner declared my death was suicide,
 I just wanted to be my dead daughter's side.

I loved the marches during the rent strikes,
 All us boys riding behind on chopper bikes,

It was brilliant there laughing with my mates,
That's where I asked Joan for our first date.

Every touch and every thrust and every kiss,
Every feud, every fight, every lip split,
Every face lost at the window of a tower block,
Every loan shark with a list of women in hock.

Every whiskey, every Valium, every cigarette,
Every couple holding hands in a kitchenette,
Every laughing child being spun in the August sun,
Every boy with a piebald horse to gallop on.

Every mother dreaming about some different life,
Every first tooth, first communion, every surgeon's knife,
Every welder, office cleaner, every unemployed,
Every girl who fought back when her dreams died.

Every young poet who wrote it out in verse:
McDonagh and MacDermott, Connolly and Pearse,
Every name scrawled on walls in each tower block,
Every face that is remembered, every face forgot;

Every life that ended here and every life begun:
The living and the dead of Ballymun.

Travel-Light

It hung on a nail in the shed, my father's Travel-Light bag,
When not being carried to the gates of Alexandra Dock

By bus from Liberty Hall, holding his clothes and alarm clock:
All the necessities in the regimented life of a ship's cook

Who paused on the gangplank to watch crane drivers load
Containers bound for Hamburg, Le Havre and Rotterdam.

How many pairs of hands caused those goods to be stowed,
With my father's crew one link in this chain of transportation?

How many men were needed before this tunnel was complete,
How many daughters helped mothers pack a holdall or Travel-Light,

How many sons carried suitcases to the corner of a street
And waved until their fathers had long passed from sight?

How many workers reached this land – which so many once left –
To ensure the everyday miracle that consignments of goods arrive

When the world is asleep, or too engrossed in its own concerns,
To be aware of factory hands packing them, of hauliers who drive

Down carriageways ruled by white lines and lined by embankments;
Of stevedores and crane drivers, forklift operators and ship-hands;

Of tunnellers striving against mudstone, struggling for entitlements,
Emerging at the Coolock interchange to yearn for distant homelands.

Five thousand workers built Dublin's Port Tunnel. Thousand more
Will watch long beads of florescent light flicker on their cab windows

As they traverse Fairview Park and East Wall inside this low tunnel
That flows beneath Marino where life continues, oblivious to them.

But behind every shipment there is the tunneller who moved earth,
Who excavated glacier deposits of boulder clay onto conveyor belts;

There is a father – like my father – forced to miss his son's birth
As he aligned the precast segments by screwing in spear bolts,

There is a planner, an engineer, a crew servicing the cutting head
That rotated every seventeen seconds through limestone rock;

There is a haulier hypnotised by cat's eyes stretching ahead;
A sailor on deck watching the lights of Dublin port contract;

There is a family in a foreign land awaiting a money transfer;
There are phone calls from Internet cafes and hostel steps;

There is a son at a corner watching his father's departure;
A patchwork of absences criss-crossing the globe at night;

An empty hook in countless homes hammered into a shed door,
Waiting to hold a rucksack, a suitcase or a battered Travel-Light.

In Memory of George Best

In one corner of our mind it remains 1969:
Frosted pavements, icy breath, yet our hands thaw

In the thrill of chasing a ball under streetlights;
Voices in the dark calling the names of Best and Law.

A drudge of decades have clogged our arteries,
Yet no matter what occurred, what we have become,

When we witness again his feint, his sheer artistry
Thousands of us are instantaneously made young.

25 November 2005

Carmen's Garden in Flanders

For Piet Chielens

Not only the ghosts of soldiers cross these battlefields
Which factories and streets long ago concreted over.
Other lives here since then were no less memorable:
Every child lost to meningitis or partner lost to cancer.

Amid the poppies their Forget-Me-Nots also grow.
Grief will never halt; her loss will remain forever.
Forget-Her-Enough to relinquish mourning though:
An evening must come when you re-enter the garden

Your loved one nurtured on land once scarred by trenches.
Lift your face into the rain and grasp these seconds
Because rain like this will never come again, seeping
Into roots of plants, into crevices thronged by finches,

Onto insect-lined stems, as life ceaselessly reawakens,
Even amidst the unassailable void death leaves behind.

First Book

For June, Deirdre & Roger

Soon my mother will return with my promised comic,
As I recuperate in her bed: a fire ablaze in the tiny grate.

Lace curtains cast light over rose-patterned wallpaper
As chanting girls play with a skipping rope at our gate.

Although ordered to remain in bed, I begin to explore.
On top of the wardrobe I find the two books we possess;

One made of gold-sprayed metal, with a coin slot and lock:
Housewife's Savings Book of the Munster & Leinster Bank.

I shake the coins inside it, then, curious, feeling grown up,
I open the single printed book that belonged to my sister.

Several pages are torn while squiggles disfigure the cover.
I struggle with strange expressions and stranger characters,

But reading it, I find myself at the window of a home in Suffolk.
The curtains are open to let me peer, with shy bewilderment,

At this incomprehensibly alien universe, but I am hooked.
I might be the stammering, the easy prey and class dunce;

But I am discovering a sphere where bullies cannot threaten:
Turing mildewed pages; I begin to inhabit two worlds at once.

The Cut

For Con Daly, Roger Bolger, Sean Considine

When the cut is decided some decades from now,
If I should prove to be the final golfer standing

I will leave for my friend a wooden tee, neatly broken:
His Indian sign left behind to mark each perfect drive.

I will leave for my brother a ball miraculously perched
On the edge of an unplayable hazard, just within bounds,

Sitting up with such incongruous temptation in the rough
That no stranger finding it could resist playing the shot.

For my brother-in-law I will leave a discarded cigarette butt
Nonchalantly smouldering on the fringe of a deserted green,

Having being tossed away to allow him to slay another par putt.

From *Night & Day: 24 Hours in the Life of Dublin* (2008)

Author's Note to *Night and Day*

'Night & Day' is a sequence of observational poems tracing the thoughts of passing commuters in a succession of mental snapshots set during the course of twenty-four hours in the life of Dublin. The full sequence was first displayed on posters in public buildings, as words and video images projected onto pavements at night and incorporated into wall murals in locations as diverse as Luas tram stops and the gable of the Cunas and Cairdeas Centre in Neilstown, north Clondalkin, which housed the local Drugs Task Force and where the poem 'Neilstown Matadors' is set. Poetry will rarely affect a broad constituency when displayed in a public space. But I was seeking the one person in five hundred who turns a familiar corner and is surprised to see a hint of their own life experience reflected back at them. These posters became my way of leaving the sort of sign I had longed for as a youth, an affirmation of the validity of seeing the world in a different light.

They were commissioned under South Dublin County Council's INCONEXT3 Percent for Art, a public art scheme which allowed me to become an observer, to journey through those streets and speculate about the thoughts of passers-by or write about strangers who stopped to tell me of their lives. These poems became the pages of a public book, left open on gable ends, displaying an invitation for local writers to join in my imaginative journey by sending me their own work written in response. My sequence was published first in the solo collection, *External Affairs*, but then also in an anthology I edited, entitled *Night & Day*. This anthology paired each poem of mine with poems written by two dozen other writers. In this way, the original audience for the poster poems also became co-authors of the resultant anthology.

On the 7 a.m. Luas to Tallaght

I never thought that the West would be like this:
Trying to sleep on the tram to Tallaght at dawn,
My mouth so dry I can no longer taste your kiss.

Swapping phrases in ten languages for tiredness,
Fellow passengers stare out, barely able to yawn:
They never thought the West would be like this.

This journey compounds every ache of loneliness.
I close my eyes, unable to stop thinking of home,
My mouth so dry I can no longer taste your kiss.

Last night on the phone I could sense your stress,
Our children no longer asking when will I come:
I never thought that the West would be like this.

To them I've become a cheque from a foreign address,
A man who builds apartments we could never own,
My mouth so dry I can no longer taste your kiss.

All day I will shovel cement, yearning to caress
Your neck with each button of your blouse undone:
I never thought that the West would be like this,
My mouth so dry I can no longer taste your kiss.

Conquistador, Pilgrim Soul

Three times I have sacrificed myself as a martyr,
Have forfeited my life so that others might escape,

Thrice I was betrayed by friends before daybreak,
Thrice I rose from the dead to reboot my computer.

This is my life, or dare I say it, my truest existence.
My other world of enduring eight hours in an office,

Before sitting here ensnared in evening rush-hour traffic,
Staring at a stranger's bumper, no longer feels realistic.

Reality only starts when I arrive home to my duplex,
To consume a microwaved dinner before the computer

While I anticipate the known unknowns that may occur,
While I decide what virtual universe I elect to inhabit,

While I prepare to commence battles against strangers,
To explore new identities or relocate in my cyber abode.

My fellow office workers think me peculiar and a loner,
But I am far from alone. A world-wide web of us

Refuse to recognise their physical restrictions and borders
On who we actually are or who we are allowed become.

I know where I belong and it is not stuck here in traffic.
Like my grandmother, I believe in a second existence,

But while she filled her afterlife with plaster cast saints
I populate mine with sinners, fantasists and dissidents.

My parents believe in the gospel of television newscasters.
'*You're only twenty-six,*' they say. '*You know nothing yet.*'

But I know that their universe is the ultimate illusion,
With every emotion rationalised and carefully packaged

And all eventualities covered by a comprehensive insurance plan.
Nobody can find me in my real world, yet I can be found by anyone

Who searches the infinite space where only I decide who I am
In my personalised second life that resonates with mythic beings.

I know the avatars who log on only as who they claim to be.
Perhaps the middle-aged man opposite me in this tailback

Interacted with me last night, flirtatiously masquerading as a girl:
But maybe this was his true essence made flesh with one click?

Maybe the lies we concocted online are the only actual truths,
Because we select these surrogate lives by our own free choice.

Only in such personas can we reveal our true colour or voice.
I was given no input into the accident of my nationality or sex

But in cyberspace I finally make these choices for myself,
Floating free of every constraint imposed on me from birth.

Tonight at my computer I can become my own creator,
Boring down into the core of good and evil in my soul,

To reveal each unsolved contradiction holding me in check:
Indivisible, indissoluble, omnificent, made whole at last.

History Viewed from a Clondalkin Supermarket Car Park

Screw all self-appointed martyrs,
Ignore their beguiling monuments:
Screw any ghosts with the neck
To impose upon their descendants
The mortgage of any emotive debt,
Any cloying duty of remembrance
That turns the past into an excuse
To hold us to ransom in the present.

Let the weight of history become as light
As a party balloon slipping from the grasp
Of a distracted child in a crowded car park.
Let it float above cars choking exit lanes
Until our tribal braves become mere specks,
So indistinct amid this skyline of cranes
That they cannot be hijacked from the grave
As tools used to justify or condemn anything.

The child watches her balloon disappear,
She does not stamp her feet or simper;
She lets the past go, being too absorbed
By all the possible futures that await her.

Neilstown Matadors

Super models would kill to be this thin.
The diet is stress, cigarettes and coffee.
My child-raising days should be done,
But somebody had to step into the breach,
Somebody had to pick up the scarlet cloak
And hold it in front of the rampaging bull.

Old spectators in the bull rings of Mexico
Pay no heed to fearless young toreadors
Who imagine themselves to be invincible.
Their interest only stirs after a fighter is gored,
Because only when he re-enters the arena
Will they witness his true test of character.

Some afternoons after school in this room,
Waiting to see the Drugs Taskforce worker,
When my granddaughter suddenly smiles,
When she looks up from her colouring book
With eyes that match my daughter's eyes,
With eyes knowing nothing yet of the danger
Of peddlers peddling needs that need to be fed,
With quizzical eyes that I would kill to protect,
She asks the question that she loves to ask:
'Gran, what did you do before you did this?'

What did I do before I took on her welfare?

I fought to raise a daughter on these streets,
I stood in queues and worked on checkouts,

I searched for my child on dangerous estates,
I stood up to debt collectors calling to my door,
When she shivered in detox I tried to nurse her,
I sold my possessions or saw them all robbed,
I cried until one night there were no tears left,
I prayed with what remained of my ebbing faith,
In time I wrapped my grandchild into my arms
And took the place of the person I loved most,
I made a nest amid the belongings I possess,
I stood up in the bull ring every time I was gored,
I watched the bulls run and I raised my cloak
Repeatedly to provide what shelter I could,
I picked myself up and wiped off the blood,
I waited at the school gate to take her hand
So that, walking home, no evil could touch her.

I don't say such things as I stroke her fingers.
Instead I say, as her eyes widen with wonder:
'Every night during your ten years in this world
As you sleep I enter the bull ring with my sword
To stand where your mother would have stood:
A gladiator standing guard, a secret matador.'

Girl, Fifteen, Walking in Ronanstown

I am walking and I shall keep walking,
Past the gangs clustered on the corners
With nothing except catcalls and jeers,

Past shuttered shops where we kissed,
Past graffiti-strewn lanes we haunted
Before his betrayal soured their magic.

I am walking past interrogating stares,
An inquisition of girls with know-all eyes.

I am Nicky-No-Name, declining all labels,
Walking tall because I know my own worth.

I refuse to look down and refuse to look back,
I shiver from the cold but feel no regret,

Because I carry my destination in my heart,
Even if I lack the words to express it yet.

Graffiti on a Corner

Each time I pause at this corner
    It unlocks a private code:
Myriad labyrinths of memories
    Flash past along the road.

The thrill of being chased, first kiss,
    First time to encounter love:
You may see a bare street corner,
    I glimpse a treasure trove.

Wedded

For Bernie

This is what I am wedded to:
The bus journey in the dusk,
Tailbacks, roadworks, queues.
Tired commuters gazing into space,
Thrown forward in our seats
Every time the driver brakes;
As inane strangers on mobile phones
Force us to eavesdrop on their lives.

The name carved on a boulder
At the entrance to our estate,
The sweep of curving rooftops,
The bicycles left on the path,
Hopscotch marked out in chalk.

The light in the kitchen window
When she gets home before me,
The bustle of pots, the radio
Blathering about the outside world;
A scent of spices as she says hello,
Busy stirring some dish at the stove.

The voice of the woman I wed,
Who makes every aspect blessed:
This kitchen, this suburban street,
This bus trip like a pilgrimage

Back to where I may finally lie
With my bride amid shoals of roofs,
Amid the vast galaxies of estates,
Amid the myriad specks of light,
In the place where I am safe,
Where I wake deep in the night
And touch her sleeping face.

The Absent Father

He is the smiling man releasing the boy's hand at the door,
Timing to the last second when he must bring him back.

He is the six days of purgatory when he tortures himself
With longing for a glimpse of his son's eight-year-old face.

He is a succession of Happy Meals and playgrounds,
An opened wallet, the questions his son cannot express,

An extra portion of fries, a man trying not to obsess
About making each moment they spend together precious.

He is the cause of confusion; a love that is boundless;
A blemish in what should be his son's fairy-tale world;

A father only snatching glimpses into the boy's life.
He is a monthly standing order, a hunter with his gun

Who lost his way out hunting, a sailor marooned at sea
Outside a Clondalkin house, awaiting his scheduled time.

He is a weekly routine, a slot allotted by a mediator,
A concerned voice unable to discern if things are all right,

He is the name that his son has learnt not to call out for:
The absence who cannot banish the boy's fears at night.

Passing Certain Housing Estates

On the night that they announce his death
Those of us who live in the homes he built
Will assemble at his ornately gated mansion.

We will carry his oak coffin on our shoulders
In a silent procession through every estate
Where he ignored bylaws and left roads incomplete.

We shall dig his grave to half its legal depth
And lower his casket as far down as it will fit,
Promising to return later and complete the task.

His coffin will be left jutting out on a slant,
And on his subsiding headstone will be writ:
'Death too has short cuts and sharp practices,
Here I lie as I left you, betrayed by empty promises.'

Flowers Mark the Spot

Flowers mark the spot
Of the stolen car's somersault.
Flowers mark the spot
Of another unprovoked assault.
Supermarket bouquets,
Barely noticed, wrapped in plastic,
Held aloft by sellotape
Where a girl sought her fix,
Where lovers found a body
Whose hands were neatly tied,
Where a driver lost control,
Where someone's daughter died.

Bouquets that disintegrate
During months devoid of sleep,
When numb parents ache
To hear again a key turn in a lock
As loved ones arrive home
Having survived the roulette of fate.

Withered flowers represent
A grief they can never articulate.

Haulier passing The Red Cow Roundabout, 11.15 p.m.

I just want to be home, is that too much to ask?

Even when asleep I see white lines, hard shoulders,
Automated cranes on foreign wharves loading ships,

I see that final container that I still have to deliver,
The one that always seems to keep me from home,

I see tailbacks and blockades and upturned wreckage,
Docksides where I smoke when sleep refuses to come.

The blonde teenage hitchhiker incessantly pulling a comb
Through her hair as she climbed up into my truck,

Strung out on heroin, falling asleep on my shoulder
With the same smile as my thirteen-year-old daughter.

Jesus of Clondalkin

Maybe Jesus is wandering these roads tonight,
Unrecognised, unacknowledged, utterly alone,

Passing half-built apartment blocks investors own,
Passing burnt-out cars, glass shards, twisted chrome,

Threading a path through Neilstown and Quarryvale,
In Dunnes Stores white socks, with his jacket torn.

Maybe we are so adrift in our own cares that we fail
To see whip marks, collapsed veins, his crown of thorns.

Possibility

Just leave yourself open to the possibility
That one dawn you wake to find your mind clear,

One dawn you win back the love you derailed,
One dawn you will kick the habit of blaming yourself.

One dawn you will wake to hear a clear signal,
A wavelength unmuffled by inference or static,

You will recognise the DJ's voice as your own
Advertising a unique extravaganza treasure hunt
Where each clue is a signpost through your past.

You will walk through a maze of sleeping estates,
Collecting golden tickets concealed amid mistakes
You made when addiction stopped you thinking straight.

That dawn, when figures emerge amidst the chaos,
You will walk forward, unafraid to embrace happiness.

The Frost Is All Over

For Tony McMahon, David Power & David Teevan

Tuning Up

In kitchens and pub corners and concert halls
Musicians gather. They open instrument cases,
Tune up, exchange greetings, gossip and yarns
Until, gradually, the noise of everyday life ceases.

At some unspoken moment they become someone other
Than who they were when walking in through the door.
Nobody mentions it, but the mood subtly alters
Just like the mood switches between two lovers

When one takes the lead, drawing the curtains tight
To initiate the change. A taut electricity in the air
Dissipating sharp words, healing perceived slights,
Suspending all cares in the expectant atmosphere.

The musicians arch their fingers, purse their lips,
Pause for one last second and then, tantalising, slow,
Fingers and lips allow the tune to find its shape
And steadily grow towards its blistering crescendo.

'Culna Dear, Don't Come Any Nearer Me...'

You can never claim to own this tune,
But, with luck, it may come to own you
For brief seconds in the midst of playing
When everything else is stripped away
Except the bare skeleton of the notes
That gradually you find a way to clothe
With emotions only music can express.

Your fingers no longer feel like your own;
You have become a servant, a medium,
Allowing a procession of ghosts to slip
Through the buttons of your accordion:
The hag with the golden sovereigns
Standing amid a white sea of bog cotton,
And the singer with a craggy Connemara face,
Closing his eyes in an American city to summon
The young lover tapping at the windowpane,
The girl chiding him, yet wanting him nearer,
Both caught up in the breathless love chase.

Seamus Ennis in Drumcondra

For Tony McMahon

I see him leave that flat we shared
And walk down Home Farm Road,
Black coat buttoned against the wind,
A countryman's hat pulled down,
And in his hand a battered case,
Containing the set of uilleann pipes
Found in fragments by his father
In a sack in a London pawnbrokers:
A jigsaw nobody else could piece together
A hundred years after they were crafted
By Coyne of Thomas Street in Dublin.

He carries his case like a secret dossier
That no passer-by could decode
As he boards a bus into the city
Unnoticed among the evening throng.
Times are hard, our flat threadbare,
He survives on tins of steak and kidney pie,
On meals that he cooks at odd hours,
When he tells yarns and truly comes alive.
There is rent to pay, a meter to be fed,
Afternoon visits to the local launderette
Nights of wind rattling the rotting windows,
When he spreads his coat over his bed.

This is the price of making music,
Of living the life for which he was born,

He is on his way that night to perform
For little pay to a meagre audience
In the back room of a Dublin pub,
With a television blaring in the lounge.

Ignoring the jarring cash register,
Three dozen people sit, transfixed,
By a set of reels learned from his father
Interlaced with grace notes and tricks
Picked up from pipers who are ghosts,
Who died recorded only by himself,
Who never learnt music, wrote nothing down,
But carried the tunes in their minds,
Knowing that with their own deaths
Dozens of nameless reels would also die.
Ennis plays with due respect for the dead,
In his one good suit, a white shirt and tie.

Recording

This is the sole recording they persuaded her to make.
Listen closely and you will hear beneath the static
The clock in her hillside kitchen, the spitting fire
Set because so many neighbours were bound to arrive,
A door opening unexpectedly, a tramp of hobnailed boots
Ushering a man in from the yard, his low voice apologetic.

And behind him, beyond the thick-set window panes,
Winter wind and rain amid the bent shoulders of trees
And, even more faintly, the hum of an engine running
To charge the batteries that power the revolving spools
Of the reel-to-reel tape machine in her gas-lit cottage,
Where she has made tea for strangers and neighbours,

Apologised for the pot-holed lane and shocking weather,
Discussed local deaths, the electric wires creeping closer,
When finally, reluctantly, with almost shy reverence,
She has taken her grandfather's fiddle from the wall,
And started to play the tunes he taught her as a girl.

Bold Doherty

Mary Ann Carolan sings in old age on the Hill of Rath,
She sings of Bold Doherty, that hard-drinking man,
She sings for her mother who taught her this song,
She sings for the collector who tracked her down,
A young man with a bouzouki from her native town,
She sings to fill out the years this song was unheard,
She sings to reflect the depth of life she has known,
She sings for a young girl who has not yet been born,
A child who late one night will hear an old woman
Sing on the radio and fall in love with the words:
A punk-haired girl who will later travel the world,
To conjure up Bold Doherty's drunken wanderlust
In a blue spotlight, white hands clasping the microphone,
A stranger in a strange time making this song her own.

'O'Neill's Cavalcade'

It takes the bones of a lifetime to learn to play,
To probe your way into the soul of the tune,
To show the notes enough respect to open up
So that a line of ninety-nine ghosts march forth:

The retreating chieftain and his cavalcade,
The moonlit ships, their white sails raised:
With unbowed swagger, vowing to return,
Defiant exiles gaze back at a shrinking land.

Sport

The sport of dancer's boots striking the floor,
The sport of hands clasped, a gasp for breath,
The flying trail of sparks from nails on stone,
The secretive slipping past crowds at the door;
The cold night air, the waving trees overhead
In sheltering ditches, in deserted city lanes,
The chase, the catch, the lingering first kiss
Under a crescent moon, the stars gargantuan,
Her dark hall door, blood pulsing with music,
Her eyes gone serious, her bedroom light dim.

Sonny Brogan's Jigs

For Tony McMahon

At eighteen you discovered how Leitrim was located,
Anonymously and miraculously, amid a labyrinth

Of small North Dublin streets of red-brick terraces,
Down which musicians slipped with instrument cases.

The old countryman welcoming you at his hall door,
A magnolia-painted parlour, ablaze with evening light,

Where every Sunday flotillas of musicians gathered
For sessions that gathered pace until late at night.

Box players from Limerick, a fiddler from Kilrush,
Student teachers like you whose concertinas were seized,

Pipers who wanted bodhráns played only with billhooks,
And *sean-nós* singers home from labouring jobs in Leeds.

The way Sonny Brogan could conjure a sense of Leitrim,
By playing unadorned sets of jigs on his accordion,

As sparse and crisp as a hillside white with frost,
As exhilarating as walking a girl home in the dark.

Candles of horse chestnut above the college walls,
Emigrants on open-backed buses bound for the boat,

College life, mysteries of bra straps and Cavan girls,
Sweat on dance club walls, Brylcreem, saxophones,

And a passport every Sunday into a different world
When musicians gathered in Sonny Brogan's home.

The Piper Patsy Touhey plays in Cohen's Variety Show, New York, 1905

Somewhere between the vaudeville skits and slapstick fare,
Amid the heat and grease-paint of Cohen's Irish emporium,

When coarse laughter stops and catcalls quieten down,
I stare towards the dark pit that contains my countrymen,

And, striping away jaunty tricks and frilly showmanship,
I play in the style of my father who died when I was ten,

Coughing blood in a tenement amid the maelstrom of Boston,
In a flat smaller than the cabin we left behind in Loughrea.

I've told stage-Irish jokes until punters can laugh no more,
I have used darting triplets to backstitch notes that soar

High in staccato pitch before lunging down towards hell,
Like those sea voyages in steerage amidst endless swells,

With no land yet in sight and a famished land left behind.
But now amid the growing silence as I stare into the pit,

I play this slow air for my father and for all my father's kind,
Who close their eyes and recognise their own grief within it.

The Frost is All Over

In memory of Seamus Ennis, piper & collector

At Christmas in the cottage bearing his name
A packed crowd sways as musicians play.
The Naul village is quiet, a sky bereft of stars
Breathes webs of frost onto windscreens of cars.
Awakened by the tunes he once collected
The bronze statue of the piper under the tree
Stirs himself, his stiff fingers elongated
As he lifts the chanter and pipes off his knee
And takes a cautious step across the square.
In his coat pocket a half-bottle of whiskey,
In his head the notes of thousands of airs
Still jostle and cling to life in his memory.

Songs collected in Irish clubs and building sites,
In Birmingham and Brixton, Battersea and Crewe;
White-shirted men softly playing the squeeze box,
Lonely men singing about the Sweet Mountain Dew
Between shifts at the Vauxhall car plant in Luton.
Men, who once laboured with asphalt and asbestos,
Rasping out final breaths in flats in Camden Town
With the district nurse their sole weekly caller;
Men who tuned to Radio Éireann in kitchenettes
Hemmed in by foreign voices through cavity walls,
Desperate to hear a fiddle amid the static and forget
The damp odour of exile and curse of loneliness.

The ghosts swarm to join him in the frosted square
Like they swarmed as boys to hiring fairs in Strabane
And queued on Dublin quays to board cattle boats

And waited at dawn in Kilburn for contractors in vans.
A lifetime of being herded and praying to be chosen,
Of pints and tin whistles shyly produced at gatherings.

Remember me, one of them begs the bronze figure,
You recorded me one December night in Wolverhampton,
You came back to my bedsit, the only soul I ever let in.
I sang with my eyes closed amid my few possessions,
And it felt like I had only to reach out through the dark
And every face I left behind would be there to touch.

Play The Bucks of Oranmore, play The Frost is All Over,
Play for ghosts eternally condemned to be The Wild Rover.
Play for those picking mushrooms in the fields of Athenry
From Estonia and Lithuania, from Lagos and Paraguay.

Remember us, Seamus, we entrusted you with song
In Yorkshire mill towns that never felt like home.
Our legions left no footprints amid the wet cement
But you drank with us and gave our songs worth
In bothies on farms in Strathclyde and Arbroath.
We wander in limbo now, the forgotten remnants
Of an army recruited from hillside and tenement
To emigrate and send home our weekly remittance.
So strap on your pipes, Seamus, as our ghosts file
To your cottage window where young musicians play
Those tunes we shyly shared with you in our exile.

'O'Neill's Music of Ireland'

When you play this air I live again in every breath,
In how you bend a note, in how our fingers overlap
A century apart, united by seemingly incomprehensible
Sets of squiggles a Chicago Police Chief jotted down
After I helped unload a cargo steamer on the wharf.

The longshoremen tipped me a wink to take a break
Because they were in awe of Chief O'Neill's uniform
And relieved that he had not come to arrest anyone.
How cold the tin whistle felt as I took it from my shirt,
Blowing away ice with a blast that seemed to summon

Fellow Irish dock workers who clustered, bewildered
That such a big brass would waste his time to record
Some inconsequential tune I had first heard as a child,
So long ago I'd almost lost the memory of being scared
At a wake until a woman soothed me, humming its air.

Some immigrants argued about the tune's real name,
Others grew angry, urging me to play a music hall song,
As if I was dragging us back to the poverty we fled from.
They stood, cowed and sullen, as if accused of a crime
Best forgotten, with my notes taken down in evidence.

The notes I played that afternoon on the freezing wharf,
The notes a woman crooned to a scared boy at a wake,
The notes a cop pressed between the pages of his book,
The notes you now play, the notes you unconsciously hum
When you pace the floor at night, soothing your infant son.

The Nomad

Always in my mind the landscape of Waterford
Awaits beyond the boundaries of foreign towns.
On childhood nights I swore one day to explore
High into the wilds of the Knockmealdowns,
To see Dungarvan, Passage East and Tramore:
Towns sounding distant and impossibly strange.

No encounter has quenched the sense of wonder
That fuelled this life of hostels and train stations,
A life spent seeking a home, yet needing to wander,
Never able to settle on one job, one lover, one abode,
Imagining always that beyond the next set of mountains,
The next foreign city block, I'll discover a narrow road

Beckoning in the dark between hawthorn bushes,
To a bend where I will stare up at an attic window,
To see a child's face looking out into the darkness,
Listening to his mother sing in the kitchen below,
His hands at the glass pane, his gaze rapturous,
Already in his mind a nomad, a wandering hobo.

From *The Venice Suite*
(2012)

Author's Note to *The Venice Suite*

This is a sequence of poems no writer would wish to write. The memories contained here are unique to me, yet the voyage of loss it charts is undertaken by thousands of people every year – sometimes with huge support, like I was privileged to have, but often in isolation and solitude.

On the evening of 25 May 2010 my wife, Bernie, collapsed without warning while swimming with one of our sons. She had shown no symptoms of ill health and was a whirlpool of energy and mischief, with no thought of death before death so cruelly thought of her. I was beside her when she died from an undiagnosed ruptured aortic aneurysm at 2 a.m. the next morning, on a trolley in the Emergency Department of Dublin's Mater Hospital. Some preliminary tests had been done amid the heaving mayhem of that place, but she was still waiting to see the doctor assigned to her.

On the following day the poet Paul Durcan – whom Bernie was hugely fond of from visits to our home – sent my sons and me his poem 'Bernie', (printed in his book, *Praise in Which I Live and Move and Have My Being*, published by Harvill Secker) which served as a prologue to this suite when originally published and now is engraved on her tombstone.

In the numbness of grief I felt certain I would never write poems again. Indeed I made no conscious effort to write anything, focussing instead on the myriad responsibilities faced by any grieving partner. I found myself writing one poem, 'Venice', which tried to ease the terror of her final moments by juxtaposing them with one of her happiest memories. I have no real recollection of writing any others, but when I undertook a sorting through the drawers in our house, eighteen months after her death, I found a multitude of scraps of paper tucked away in different places: barely legible handwritten notes quickly scribbled on torn pages from copybooks or the backs of envelopes.

They were not poems as such, but seemed to be notes left to myself during different stages of that first dark year of mourning. Although the concluding 'Where We are Now' was written later, by and large the redrafting of these poems was not contemporaneous with the emotions they express. They are reconstructions of those raw emotions eighteen months on – finishing the poems that I would have written had I been in any fit state to actually compose a poem when halted at traffic lights or turning a corner at night to first spy a bedroom light not on.

There were far more scraps of paper than there are finished poems here, but I was conscious of a need to write not as many poems as possible but as few. Others fragments might have made better poems, but no grieving partner can ever say everything they need to say. Like an archaeologist trying to reconstruct only what they can be certain about, I needed to focus on those fragments that best yielded themselves up to the transformations of being shaped into verse with whatever experience I have gleaned in almost forty years of writing.

Like anyone who suffers bereavement, I will never be the person that I previously was, because when you love someone a part of you dies with them. Nor indeed am I necessarily still the person who scribbled the first drafts of these poems, so shell-shocked that I often have no recollection of doing so. But reshaping those scraps of paper into poems allowed me to confront that initial year of grieving and – in so much as people do actually move on – to try and imagine myself into a different life as the different person that I am now.

As I say, these particular memories are unique to me, but the underlying emotions are not. Thousands of people every year articulate the emotions expressed here with far greater eloquence in the silence of their hearts than I have managed to do in reconstructing thoughts first scribbled down on whatever scrap of paper came to hand.

Dermot Bolger
September 2012

In memory of
Bernie Bolger
3rd July 1958 – 26th May 2010

Venice

After her confused terror in those heart-stopping seconds
In the squalid maelstrom of an Accident & Emergency ward,

Amid stretchers and trolleys and policemen guarding drunks,
Amid paper cones to vomit into, amid spasms and pleas
For some doctor to recognize that her throat was killing her,

I need her to wake suddenly and find herself on that train at dawn
Which terminated by accidental miracle at a station in Venice,

When she was nineteen on a Transalpino student rail pass,
Seeing unlimited European cities in a limited number of days,
Sleeping on carriages and benches, arrested for bathing topless

Off remote rocks lit by Catalonian sun and Franco's shadow;
Seeing countries she always dreamt of, encountering strangers
Who strummed guitars on beaches. Forever losing her purse,

Her rucksack, her limited and yet untethered sense of direction;
Careering excitedly down the concourse of some Hauptbahnhof,
Awash with platforms and destinations and not a second to spare

To board the right train shunting out into a landscape now twilit:
Distant lights, dark farmland, a coat pillowing her head as she slept,
Thinking herself travelling in one direction but instead being swept,

While she curled in blissful sleep without any dreams of the future,
Inadvertently closer to that metropolis she had always longed to see.

After her panic at being unable to breathe, her frantic death-gasp,
I need her to wake up slowly to a sense of being encircled by water,

To sleepily read the station nameplate, barely able to believe her eyes
At being transported to this destination she instinctively recognized;

To walk forth from the dawn-lit station and to find herself transfixed,
With her infinite childlike wonder, at the incandescent mystery of it.

All Hallows Library, 31 August 2010

Jack B. Yeats's Painting, *Grief* (1951)

Someday each one of us will stand amid this:
Indigo blue shards of grief, a blistering deluge
Of mustard flecks of rain that seal us within
A bewildered state which we desperately need –
Yet so desperately fail – to make any sense of.

The Empty Car

I never thought of it in this light before,
But I always knew precisely who I was:

On interminable late-night drives home
From public readings in remote towns;

On evenings sprinting through airport terminals
To catch the last flight closing at a distant gate;

In supermarkets, texting to ask what we needed,
Hoping to surprise you with a gift of chocolate;

On afternoons rushing out of television studios,
So anxious to beat the traffic and reach home

That you would laugh, wiping make-up off my face;
On vacating solitary rooms where I sat until sunset,

Engrossed in intricate parallel universes of fiction;
On daily whiskey runs to console my ailing father;

During afternoons on sidelines when our son kept goal;
Evenings in playgrounds; expeditions to hardware stores;

In freezing Octobers when twilight lasted just long enough
For golfers on the eighteenth green to read sloping putts.

In whatever roles financial necessity required me to enact,
Juggling responsibilities, trying to buy us space and time,

I still knew my exact identity in my soul's unalterable core:
I was the man perpetually rushing home to be with you,

Hoping your light was still on as you completed a crossword,
Exhausted or exuberant, drawing me back into my real world.

Because that bedside was where my chameleon life ceased
And I simply became again the husband you had chosen,

With all other personas suspended as I became complete
By chatting or spooning into you or just stroking your feet.

*

Tonight as I turn from Mountjoy Square onto Belvedere Place,
Slowing at traffic lights intersecting the North Circular Road,

I realise for the first time I'm no longer a man driving home
To the woman he loves with infuriation, passion, tenderness.

I am robbed not only of my future but my life's purpose.
I feel invisible, passing cyclists, four girls chatting in a car,

Amazed that none of them glance out, at how they can miss
The enigma that the vehicle alongside them is driverless,

Because how can I be someone without you to drive home to?
The traffic lights change, the motorist finally glances across:

The reflection she sees through this windscreen is only as real
As light travelling from a burnt-out star that no longer exists.

Fingal Driving Range

From the dark car park where you used to sit
To check all your texts and voice messages,
Fantasias of white balls trace solitary orbits
Across a floodlit arc of sky above the rooftop,
Like silent souls failing to ascend into heaven.

Warmth

In this dream I know that you are dead,
Yet you allow me touch your inner thigh,

Warm as life but with a hairline scratch
To break the silky expanse of elegant skin.

I know my hands must stray no further,
Because they would only encounter emptiness:

You have sent this sole segment of yourself
As a parting gift, a remembrance of how it felt

To be at one with another soul inside an embrace:
Two lives shared, one heartbeat, two breaths.

You allow me these six inches of skin to touch
So that when I wake in the parched ache of dawn

I will still retain some aftertaste of the warmth
That stems from being spooned into a lover's flesh.

*

After a loved one dies there are duties to complete:
The daily ruse of tasks used to keep grief at bay.

But nights lack itineraries to camouflage the void
Where desolation surges it to displace sleep,

Where regrets congeal like stalactites on ceilings,
Where I confront the fact that part of me also died

In the pandemonium of a hospital Emergency Ward,
With staff too busy restraining junkies and drunks

To diagnose the scared patient in sodden swimwear
Dying from an aneurysm on an ambulance stretcher.

Some nights I drink enough to ensure I blackout
Into a pit devoid of dreams about our shared past.

Yet at dawn my subconscious recommences its tricks:
We meet by chance and amiably chat in some corridor

Until an inconsequential remark reminds me you are dead
And jolts me awake into the nightmare of bereavement.

But in this dream you send only six inches of yourself
Which I may kiss and serenely caress for these brief seconds,

Totally aware that I am asleep and must soon awaken,
Conscious you have died but I am somehow being allowed

The consolation of stroking your skin one final time
Before I arise to resume being the actor I've become:

A walking ghost who fulfils contractual commitments,
A poet now only attuned to the iambic pentameter

Of spin dryers and washing machines in our shed,
Coping with school lunches, ironed shirts, book lists,

Acutely aware of the sons whom you blessed me with,
Conscious of every twist that our lives did not take,

Acutely alone except for the after-touch of a ghost
Who came to me in a bed where we once made love.

Lines Transcribed from Latvian

In the topmost attic berth of this obsolete retreat,
Where shutters tremble from the gale-force gusts
That comb back branches amid the darkening earth,
Before battering exposed windows and brickwork:
I lie awake, held captive by that loneliest sound
In a room without a soul to put my arms around.

That Which is Suddenly Precious…

… Crease marks where you folded hotel receipts;
The *to-do* list pinned onto your bedroom mirror;

A moisturiser jar with your fingerprint still visible;
Old concert ticket stubs, a cherished dinner menu

Stowed away in the ornate box on the dressing table
That served as your child-like pirate treasure chest.

A hotel drinks bill after viewing a film with friends,
Scribbled notes I left with flowers, birthday cards,

A yellow golf-ball I unearthed from deep rough
Knowing you'd like the smiley face scrawled on it.

The casual words with which I coaxed you outside
To sunbathe while I blithely cooked our final meal,

Watching you relish sunlight on your naked back.
A million words and times we exchanged no words,

Quarrels over slights eventually resolved by kisses.
Companionable silences shared in our back garden

Till howls from unattended dogs forced us indoors.
Footprints on a Wexford beach, cycling Dublin streets;

A notebook crammed with tips to improve your golf.
Such inconsequential mementos made consequential:

A thousand artifacts to sort through; discard or keep,
From a life that has inadvertently become itemised:

Each scribbled message now an historical footnote.
The thousand things that I would now wish to say,

The thousand things I would now wish to change,
The leave-takings to be confronted in every drawer:

The unanswerable, the unknown, the unexpressed;
The keenest ache of loneliness just after I wake;

The fact I knew you intimately for a quarter-century;
The mystery that perhaps I barely knew you at all,

The realization that nothing in life remains permanent
Except for old love notes stored in a treasure chest,

With their unalterable intent, their fixed sentiment
Rendered, with one stroke, into the past tense.

Candle

I cannot expect your ghost to be summoned
On every occasion on which I light a candle.

For twenty-five years I was a part of your life,
Yet I was never the sum total of your life.

Your ghost must surface and wane as you will:
Loitering in corners at unannounced moments

When I am utterly oblivious to your presence,
Before you disappear back into previous worlds

Which exist for me only as Polaroid photographs
In albums you packed amid multitudinous suitcases

On the night we moved into our apartment together:
That night you grew upset because I arrived on my bike

With two plastic bags strung together on the cross-bar,
As if I was not taking seriously our entry into a shared life.

I was deadly serious that night and over the years since,
Both as a carefree young man with too few possessions

And a widower besieged by everything we accumulated:
Suitcases stacked in attics, boxes squeezed under beds,

Alcoves crammed with memories I seem unable to cast aside;
Our shared past catalogued in casually stacked photographs:

Each negative made precious, yet also rendered worthless.

How much do I hold onto and what should I discard?

You do not live on in suitcases or in my troubled dreams:
Even before death you had grown independent of me,

Had gathered your strength to rise from your sick bed
And become again the person you were before we met,

The girl inside the pages of those old photograph albums
Laughing with unidentified figures, friends I never knew.

Do you live only in photographs or exist in some sphere
That I lack the vocabulary or intuition to comprehend?

I imagine you in a white dress on a Swiss mountaintop,
Unencumbered by worries, freer than I ever knew you.

But perhaps you still fret over earrings, elegantly dressing
To spend your days flitting between realms and locations,

On some journey that occasionally transports you back
To this room in the tiny house we once called home,

Where a solitary man sits typing beside a lit candle;
The youth who cycled to you with just two plastic bags

Tied to his bike because, miraculously, he had found you
And consequently needed no other possession on earth.

So Many First Times…

The first time you depart an airport with no one to fly home to:
First time you turn a street corner to find no kitchen light on:
First night away you realise you have no one to text *Sleep tight*:
The first time you sense how so many inconsequential moments
Were momentous for last being shared with someone you loved.

Little Xs

Unexpectedly this October afternoon, the telescope turns,
I see myself, made small again, through its objective lens:

I am not the widower, who recently buried my wife,
Nor the dutiful son who kept vigil while my father,
Like a punch-drunk boxer, fought to out-fox death,

Demented and enraged, hands trapped in cartoon gloves
To stop him pulling out the tube to his morphine pump.

Today we clear the house where he lived for sixty years.
In the bedroom where I was born, my siblings recall

How, as children, their only clue to my birth occurring
Behind this closed door were anxious instructions to pray.

When we open up the attic we discover the suitcase
My mother packed for her last trip into hospital:

A wash-bag and talc, clothes she never got to wear home,
A purse crammed with prayers and the folded letter
I wrote, as a ten-year-old, for my sister to bring into her.

I spend one page telling her how good I'm being, then cram
Three pages with scrawled Xs – each one to represent a kiss.

Last week a granddaughter she never knew sang on stage,
Luminous and radiant, in a band named Little Xs for Eyes.

For four decades in a letter in a purse in a suitcase in this attic
These galaxies of Xs were the banished eyes of a bewildered child.

But – unfolding them – I see myself stare out at who I am now,
Across this life I could never have envisaged as I scrawled
Untidy Xs for a woman I last saw smiling from a hospital bed,

Who sealed them in her purse when nurses shaved her head
In preparation for the operation she would never recover from:

Praying that one day I might open her purse and be surprised
To find my Xs returned to me: big Xs for kisses, little Xs for eyes.

Other People's Grief

1950s Dublin: two girls sit silently on an open-backed bus,
Winter coats draped over their laps so that the conductor,

Sauntering downstairs to collect their fares, will not notice
The tiny infant's coffin cautiously concealed on their knees:

The wooden box their hands cradle with covert tenderness,
En route to Glasnevin Cemetery's unmarked angels' plot.

The journey never revealed to future husbands or children:
The journey they never dare refer to, even with each other:

This ache that might have allowed daughters to decipher them:
The unutterable weight of that small box carried to their deaths.

Christmas Eve, 2010

Only once did the whole thing make sense:
Christmas Eve, forcing open our back door,
Wedged tight by the piled weight of snow,
To step forth into a night silence so austere
That it seemed to belong in no living world.

Grotesque stalactites of glistening ice hung
From drainpipes, guttering and window sills:
No traffic noises, no human voices, no birdsong,
With every songbird starved or frozen to death.
Even the dogs next door who tormented you in life,

Snarling furiously each time you ventured to our shed,
Had been silenced for days, transplanted elsewhere.
Students and migrant workers had vacated their flats
In the partitioned fiefdoms of landlords along our street.
Beyond our sleeping sons, where was the next living soul?

Holding onto the fence, anxious not to slip amid snow
So compacted that my feet could not touch the ground,
I carried a basket of clothes through the Antarctic cold,
Hoping the washing machine in our shed still functioned.
I stood beneath overhanging branches of an invasive pine

That could barely bear the weight of luminous snowflakes.
And, as I paused, with each breath as visible as ectoplasm,
I could hear my heartbeat – the only sound in the quietude
That colonized Dublin: flights grounded, roads impassable,
Cars abandoned, passengers sleeping in airports terminals.

This incessant freeze made no sense. But for one moment,
Clutching the fence for support, holding the basket tight,

It made absolute sense if I let myself deconstruct each clue:
I was Nicole Kidman in *The Others*, too stubborn to realize
That, six months ago, it was I who had actually died, not you.

The unprecedented landscape was not real, crystallized snow
Sparking in diamond clusters and wedging cars doors inoperable.
In wherever the real world existed, you were doing domestic chores
In a Christmas made difficult by being the first since my death.
Why had I not grasped this simple fact? These nightmare months

Were figments of my dying brain, a narrative forged to make sense
Of the onset of death. For one relieved moment in the eerie glare
Radiating from rooftops and lawns, besieged by oppressive silence,
I truly believed this scene could only be a landscape of the dead.
I felt no grief or regret, just a dull curiosity as to what occurs next.

Then I wrenched open the shed door, glad the machine still worked.
Loading clothes into the cylinder reconciled me to my senses:
I was alive, though perished, and our sons needed clean shirts.
Cautiously I edged my way back up through that humdrum terrain
Because only your charmed laugh could truly render it magical.

The Final Three Words

If I try to recall everything, everything will be lost:
If I try to make sense of it, I will lose my reason.

One morning I shall wake and finally comprehend
The futility of applying logic to resolve the illogical.

Trying to analytically piece together unverifiable
Thoughts will only propel me down cul-de-sacs,

This approach is too blunt for any true cartography
Of the inexhaustible inner space of a woman's heart.

A quarter-century should be sufficient to know somebody:
But if I had slipped under your skin as a micro-organism,

A loosened sliver of bacteria on the pathologist's blade,
I'd have found myself adrift – a jettisoned space probe

Propelled past elliptical galaxy clusters I never know existed,
Towards the dark matter of dreams you could not express.

I knew you more intimately than any other human being,
But this doesn't allow me to claim to know you outside in:

We all withhold parts of ourselves, even from ourselves;
Those irrational contradictions we can never articulate.

I am lost, sweetheart, a satellite cruising through the debris
Of your stopped heart, bereft of gravitational pull or any purpose

Except to keep recording ghost images from the quarter-century
That unspools beneath me, with each rotation of the earth,

From this perspective, where inner and outer space merge,
Where I drift within you, yet timelessly float through the cosmos

So that I find myself gazing down as you lock your bicycle
That night you met me at Trinity in those tight white jeans.

We shelter beneath trees, shield one another with kisses in a storm
While lightning ignites a ribcage of skyline above a Wicklow forest.

I see our bicycles descend mountain slopes in torrential rain.
I watch us wake in a winter dawn, bodies so tightly intertwined

That twilight darkens our apartment by the time we finally rise.
I see myself run through ice-white streets to wave down a taxi

The night your waters broke; I grip your hand and can only kiss
Your sweating forehead as you cry out: immersed in childbirth.

I see laughter and silences, nights of exhaustion, tempers flaring
When the pensioner next door blares her television until dawn.

I see your charmed smile at tiny treats: a bar of Turkish Delight,
A box of coloured golf balls left with handwritten instructions

To take them out next time some woman was rude on the course,
So they could be a reminder that three men at home loved you.

I see the things we expressed and things we never got time to say,
I see our life spin faster, kaleidoscopes of seasons starting to blur

Into each other, revolving so fast that they crease to make sense:
Loose ends, hurts, differences, a thousand reconciling embraces.

Can I capture the woman I once thought I knew so intimately
Or chart with certainly the meaning of the totality of our lives?

All I know is that in my bedside locker I keep the small envelope
You slipped into my bag once when I was departing on a trip,

Containing a photo of you, taken after making love in a Mayo wood.
Our bicycles lie nearby. You smile, muffled up in an old scarf,

Uncaring how you looked back then, unaware you looked beautiful
And utterly, radiantly, yourself: the girl with whom I fell in love,

Unburdened by affectation, ecstatic at having miraculously found
The soul-mate you felt so despondent to be briefly separated from

That you discreetly tucked this envelope into my overnight bag,
With three words scrawled in biro in your unblemished hand,

In case I should ever doubt their enduring truth: *I Love You.*
The three words you repeated as I kissed your damp forehead

On a hospital trolley: both of us terrified and terrifyingly unaware
You were about to breathe your last. Nothing unresolved matters:

I need no grief manuals or holy texts to fathom the inexplicable,
Once I keep faith with the words you left with your photograph

For me to find, lest I should ever despair or need to call upon
Their simplicity to sustain me, lying awake at night: *I Love You.*

Where We Are Now

Three years have passed since a day of incessant snow
That halted at midnight, when I ventured with our boys
Through the unchained park gates opposite our house

Into a white moonscape untainted by footstep or bird claw.
Squadrons of swollen clouds impeded any moon or starlight,
Allowing an eerie luminosity to emanate from the ground.

Branches overburdened, benches twice their natural size:
Each everyday object transformed into a source of light.
The ordinary made wondrous: rendered gleaming at midnight.

We three raced home to try and lure you from your bed
To share in our witnessing of this miraculous spectacle,
But you complained you were sleepy, snuggled down,

You waved aside each entreaty as we begged you to come:
'*Not tonight,*' you said, '*not now, but I promise the next time*'.

None of us could have conceived that when such snow next fell
It would cover your grave for weeks, leaving us shell-shocked,
Mutely comforting each other in mourning your absent radiance.

*

Two years after your death I have finally built our extension,
With six feet of balustraded decking, five steps above the garden.
Our sons have converted it into an impromptu amphitheater.

Tonight its recessed lights are abetted by the colossal supermoon
That occurs each twenty years, when its orbit is nearest the earth.

Guitars and a mandolin have been brought out to accompany songs
Composed by your sons and their friends, interspersed with old tunes

You would love to hear, as lads pass around long-necked foreign beers.
We three have known grief; have carried coffins thrice in two years,

But tonight is serenely beautiful: this is where we are, in this moment
That cannot be repeated. You'd love to sit here, but if you were in bed

I would need to plead and coax you to get dressed and wander down,
With you protesting: '*Not tonight, not now, but I promise the next time.*'

*

Next time such a supermoon occurs our sons will be forty and forty-one:
I may be a pensioner of seventy-three or be long since deceased.

I don't know what or where I will be, I am robbed of all certainty,
Liberated from trying to predict the future or shield you from it.

I know only the single lesson we have been taught by your death:
There is no next time; no moment will replicate the wonder of now.

I feel you have moved on and I possess no desire to hold you back:
But, just this once, don't say '*Not tonight, but I promise the next time*';

Don't argue or prevaricate, but let your ghost come and sit, unnoticed,
On the wooden steps of this moonlit deck that throbs with song.

Be with us, for the eternity of this supermoon, as guitars change hands:
See what fine sons you blessed the world with; what good friends

They have summoned around them with music and chilled beer.
Two years on and this is where we are: mourning you deeply still,

Yet moving on, as we must move on: our eldest finished his degree,
Our youngest immersed in college life, their dad in a battered hat

Joining the gathering briefly to sit and share shots of Jägermeister.

We don't know where you are, but we are finding ourselves again.
I don't know if ghosts exist or just a welcoming emptiness awaits:

All I know is that, if you were here, dragged protesting from bed,
You would love to hear these songs, these subtle guitar riffs.

So, whether your ghost sits here or not, I want you to know we are okay
As I call you back to be with us one last time and then let you depart.

While We Sleep

In memory of Roger Bolger Senior,
b: 17th May 1918, Wexford
d: 20th April 2011, Dublin

While we sleep they are slipping beyond our reach –
Our elderly parents, frail aunts, grandfathers –

They are dressing themselves, opening doors in the night,
Venturing out in search of the first home they possessed;

Padding across motorway intersections in slippers in the dark,
Shuffling past shopping centres, hulls of lit-up office blocks.

We may be scared but they know where they are voyaging
Amid their endless confusion as to whether it is night or day,

Amid the terror they feel as they sense their brains capsizing,
They are walking back towards the reassurance of first memory:

The bedrock which for decades got obscured by pressing concerns,
Preoccupied with the business of surviving the business of life.

But now the clutter of middle years has been hacked away,
Reunited with themselves, unhurriedly, with vision unimpaired,

They are shuffling their way back to the streets of their birth,
Skirting carriageways, concourses, each neon-lit underpass.

They are any age and yet they have grown beyond age,
They have become absences in our lives, demanding our care,

Yet at the same time oblivious to us. We confuse them,
Disconnected from the landscape in which they are young.

We see shrunken figures in dressing gowns on Zimmer frames
But they are children sent to do a message, an errand of trust.

How can my father be ninety-two as he walks through Wexford Town,
Knocking on neighbours' doors, stopping cloth-capped strangers,

Sent out to seek the loan of a good book for my grandfather to read:
A novel with sufficient heft and depth and intelligence to distract

A compositor sick of back proofing racks of letterpress newsprint,
Who wants to lose himself in a journey through unfamiliar streets?

A quiet man who would be led astray by old age into the County Home,
Where he waited for the books he sent his young son to seek years before.

Gentle grandfather, Republican typesetter, drinker on Ram Street,
Your vigil is over at the barred window of that Enniscorthy asylum,

Your son is coming with your treasured copy of the *Observer*
That he dutifully collects from the Dublin train every Sunday morning,

With a Canon Sheenan novel, with H. G. Wells and Chesterton,
With Charles Dickens, Edgar Allen Poe and Patrick McGill,

He got distracted from his errand during decades in ship's cabins,
Grieving his wife's death, becoming a connoisseur of loneliness.

But now he emerges through the far side of such struggles,
He has left his front door open, every light on deck aglow,

He shuffles on a busted hip, clutching a vast armful of books,
Knowing only that somewhere between Finglas and Wexford,

Between the century of his birth and the one where he dies
He will encounter his own father, equally ancient, equally young.

His father will be pleased with the books, the errand fulfilled.
So while we fret for him adrift in such dangerous depths,

Unable to steer between tides of remembrance and despair,
A part of him siphons free from the confused husk who phones

Moments after we leave his house to ask why nobody ever comes:
The part that walks, beyond our remit, towards his dead father.

Even if we could follow them, they would be too engrossed to care
For the distraction of strangers like us who are not yet even born:

We would be intruding on a father and a son strolling back from town
To the Green Street terrace that is the first and the last home they share.

New Poems (2013–2015)

Night in the House on Dawson Street

No metropolis ever truly sleeps in the night.
But one inconspicuous fleeting moment occurs,

One most split of seconds when noise dissipates
And every thoroughfare appears to hold its breath

To soak in the abundance of the day it just beheld.
All the lives played out, chances and second-chances

Bestowed on denizens and citizens and fleeting visitors
Who traverse these streets in a rich continuum of life

That ceases only for this instant when heartbeats slow,
When dying patients breathe their last in muted wards

And even sparrows hidden in foliage on St Stephen's Green
Forget to fret about predators perpetually stalking them.

Dublin's stonework has breathed life in: now the walls exhale,
Perhaps in every building, but nowhere more so than this house

That for three hundred years has stood, with arrayed windows
Looking out onto the street to allow the street to look back in.

Over time other houses change their purpose, their *raison d'être* –
A vanquished parliament chamber demoted to a countinghouse,

A Duke's palace commandeered as an oireachtas for the people.
But at its core this house remains unaltered. This is our house:

It is us instead who change, generation bequeathing generation:
Hems shortening on skirts; drainpipe trousers; winkle-pickers;

The miraculous apparitions of shapely ankles at tram stops;
Newsboys contracting rickets, racing barefoot through dung;

Clamorous cries of street traders; unexpected cries of rebellion;
The cry of a mother afflicted by the famishment of her children;

The cry of a carriage driver, his whip spurring his master's horse;
Cries from pie-sellers, punk rockers, proselytisers and protesters;

From native speakers of Gaelic, Polish, Ilocano, Igbo and Cant.
The whisper of a lover who dared risk an intimate endearment

Which led on to a fingertip caress, to a first tentative kiss
On the pavement, outside this house that Joshua Dawson built,

When two souls were poised, hesitant about whether to commit
To the vast unknowability of the future, the supernova starburst

Which led to children and great-grandchildren, all blissfully unaware
That their existence emanated from one embrace on Dawson Street.

This is the true history of a city, the patchwork of private moments
So momentous in consequence as to be embedded in the brickwork

Of this building which has been such a constant backdrop in our lives
That we rarely recognise how incorporated our stories are in its
     history too.

But now, during this epicentre of the night, step through its door:
Thousands have already done so, thousands more will follow us.

Access was not always so easily gained. More than ornate woodland
Once separated this house from the city's disenfranchised populace.

Oligarchies of Protestant merchants kept these rooms the preserve
Of guilds of paint-stainers, cutlers, stationers, hosiers and tanners;

Aldermen who profited from pirated editions of London almanacs,
Printers of sermons and speeches, importers of patent medicines;

Fellowships of felt-makers and brewers; smiths of hallmarked silver;
Mounted yeomen honoured for having hunted down barefoot rebels;

Prohibitors of Catholic tradesmen whose loyalty might be suspect;
Cautioners against excessive usage of spirituous liquors by commoners.

Haberdashers who conjured the finest silken and worsted stockings
Gathered here to feast on turtle and toast their citadel within a city

That roused its strength to knock at this door to the beat of reform:
Mass rallies demanding repeal, emancipation and a new franchise

Based not on one creed but a flawed plutocracy of property rights.
This remained a house for the rich, but cracks appeared in windows

When the disenfranchised formed a battering ram whose blows echoed
Through the Oak Room and Round Room and up the ornate staircase.

Leopold Bloom was right in this city that mocked him. In this house
At least the revolution truly came on the due instalments plan.

Rateable valuations set high at ten pounds to exclude the poor,
But valuations are like mercury and the mercury will always fall

When windows are burst open to let a changing wind blow asunder
The crystal prisms of chandeliers as if they were dandelion spores.

Here Comes Everybody: from Alfie Byrne to Humphrey
     Chimpden Earwicker;
From clandestine cabinet meetings to *céilí*-goers enjoying snowball fights.

Pause on the bend of these stairs and you will hear the whispers
Of discordant voices raised to dissect a treaty, clause by clause.

A red-robed liberator still strides through rooms where previously
The only Catholics allowed were servants with bowed heads.

A rebel's widow sits on the steps, the first lady Lord Mayor
Refusing to enter until a foreign queen's portrait is ousted.

Listen to the sound of sofas being dragged from the drawing room
To let a rebellious City Council assemble on makeshift seating

In the Round Room where a rebel Dáil has declared independence
With most members detained at His nonplussed Majesty's pleasure.

Ghost footsteps of children flit across floorboards on the landing,
Unmindful of adult arguments tersely debated in rooms below,

Or else they peer through spiral-turned balusters on the stairs
As ladies arrive in herringbone corsets concealed under ballgowns

Or multitudinous deputations throng the entrance hall with petitions:
Seeking to solicit funds, signatories, reprieves or Mayoral intervention.

The Tolka is in flood: an elderly man like a ghost from another era
Leaves his sickbed to travel by open-back bus and don his chain

To orchestrate the collection of blankets, clothes, half-crowns, foodstuffs.
Dispensing sweets to children, he coughs his last into a handkerchief.

The North Strand is in flames; tenements collapsing in Church Street.
This doorbell is a conduit for discontent, for entreaties to chair
   crisis talks,

Or it is rung by a Mayor's teenage daughter, late home from a dance,
Her boyfriend kissing her on the steps and quickly releasing her hand,

Perturbed by the duality of this public residence being a private home.
These rooms once lit by tallow dips; by candles coaxed from beeswax

Or crystallised whale oil; by self-trimming braided cotton wicks
That flickered when ghosts passed; by paraffin lamps and gaslight;

By electricity and by daylight when cleaners will soon raise the blinds
To let its unheralded staff sweep and tend and prepare to usher in

The one-hundred-and-nine-thousandth, five-hundred-and-
   first morning
When this house will be a public and private space, when multitudes

Will pass with hardly a glance at this abode, which learnt to become
Whatever the city needed it to be: debating chamber, makeshift Dáil,

Dance hall where girls whirled in chiffon, cauldron where a
   Lord Mayor
Tried to intercede between inflexible employers and locked out workers.

But leave this house now: slip back onto thoroughfares that begin to stir,
Unaware of their momentary torpor; sparrows in St Stephen's Green

Shaking their beaks, aware again of predatory dangers; taxi drivers
Stepping from cars at silent ranks to stretch their limbs and greet

The hint of dawn above streets that are truly our streets, owned
By us – the Freeman and Freewoman of this municipality of Dublin

That keeps expanding with new suburbs and accents, but is colonised
By new guilds under glass domes more magnificent than cathedrals,

Whose concourses can never replace the public spaces where citizens
Can exercise their right to linger and not be labelled as consumers.

Let no one ever restrict these streets, spiderwebbed by alleyways
That all weave routes back to this house which Joshua Dawson built.

May we exercise our right to congregate here, to protest or converse
In the shadow of the mansion on the street that belongs to all of us.

Written on the 300th anniversary of Dublin's Mansion House, 2015

The Stolen Future

In memory of those children killed during the 1916 Rising

Perhaps for just one moment we can give them back
The singular precious gift pilfered from them all:

Let their personalities break free from the random fact
That braids them together, children eternally trapped

Inside a dry inventory of names: incidental casualties,
The unforeseen yet highly foreseeable collateral damage,

The flotsam invariably beached by the neap tide of history.
Startled youngsters racing between tenement doorways,

Inquisitive and naïve, famished and foraging for bread
Or some trace of a straying brother or sister. Dumbstruck,

Unable to comprehend how familiar streets and laneways
Metamorphosed into killing zones. The two-year-old girl

Slain by a bullet while cradled in her mother's arms
On a pavement marked out in chalk lines for hopscotch.

The two-year-old boy, skull split asunder by a mounted lancer,
As a petrified mother wheeled his pram down Church Street.

The teenage girl annihilated by a bullet ricocheting through a door
When rebels invaded her family's cabin to evade machine-gun fire.

The thirteen-year-old shot at her window on Haddington Road;
The twelve-year-old who expired from shock as he haemorrhaged

While being propelled in a handcart towards Jervis Street Hospital;
The sixteen-year-old boy butchered by soldiers in a tenement room,

Beseeching them to spare his father who shares his unmarked grave;
The unidentified infant, her remains unclaimed in the City Morgue.

Immature bodies interred in wooden crates, their faces kept vivid
Only for so long as elderly siblings stayed alive to remember them.

But just once let them emerge from chrysalises to blossom forth
Into the stevedores, coopers and clerks they would have become;

The newly-weds transporting furniture to Cabra by horse and cart
Or hosting a wedding breakfast for friends before taking the boat

In search of factory work and new lives in the English midlands;
The soccer player who broke his leg playing for St James's Gates

And married the shy nurse who attended him; the sad-eyed child
Who would only have lived a few years before coughing her last

In Crooksling Sanatorium for Consumptives; the hardchaw drinker
Who never let anyone glimpse the guilty love he carried in his heart;

The char who skivvied for a snooty bitch of a Glasnevin mistress;
The effervescent free spirit who painted seams of nylon stockings

On her legs with an eyebrow pencil before setting out to dance
In Dublin's Crystal Ballroom or the pulsating Ritz in Manchester

Where, bewitched by its revolving stage, she accepted a first cigarette,
Unaware that forty years later throat cancer would cause her death.

They are gone. We cannot retrieve such futures that never occurred.
But with no one left to remember, can we just once close our eyes

To imagine, instead of bone being shattered into smithereens by bullets,
A more slow-mo explosion, like the plop of one water drop on a pond

Or the way that a star splinters asunder, its shattered particles
Spiralling off to become new planets, commencing distinctive orbits.

Such stellar eruptions never occurred: the heady kisses and sperm rush
That would set in motion an infinitely expanding galaxy of descendants

All of whose lives were extinguished by stray bullets in the crossfire
That felled a young boy desperate to get home across Portobello Bridge,

That slew a stonemason's apprentice before his fourteenth birthday,
That caused boilermen and brass finishers, washerwomen and widows

To walk through shattered streets and gaze down at opened graves
Into which these stolen futures were lowered; minor postscripts

Of revolution, small narratives with arbitrary endings too truncated
To be threaded into narratives of remembrance or commemoration,

Being bereft of symbolism, ill-fitted to chronicles of sacrificial rebirth.
Deaths that neither side wished to claim, inconsequential consequences

Of commands issued by others, abridged chapters of unwritten books.
Offspring never remembered in sculpture or street names or verse;

Only in the dying breath of parents, tongues loosened by morphine
Or by endorphins triggered when oxygen is cut off from the brain,

Glimpsing their children, dressed again as they were on that day
When their absence became a permanent presence in their lives.

2015

'Whatever Happened To Francis Stable?'

Not absolutely forgotten or bereft of companionship,
Six decades after London critics lauded his early books;

During his final years his phone beeped once a week
To faithfully punctuate the long Tuesday evening silence

With a text from Greyhound Domestic Waste Services
Reminding him which colour bin to leave out for collection:

Black for waste, green for papers, brown for recycling.
He received occasional callers: antiquarian book hucksters,

Cognisant that his signature added value to a first edition;
A designated nurse who ticked him off her monthly roster;

Intrepid trekking academics, anxious to complete some footnote,
Not about his novels, but his reminiscences of a Nobel laureate.

They brought cheap wine and reinforced his embarrassment
At broken kitchen appliances and his unkempt appearance.

Only she did not judge him, his Greyhound girl, his unseen Juliet
Whose text reassured him that life still possessed one weekly task,

To subdivide all that remained into three shades of loneliness:
Brown for leaves, black for waste, green for long-rejected manuscripts.

This title is from the opening line of Ethel Mannin's 1948 novel,
Late Have I Loved Thee, *whose central character was believed to be
based on the Irish novelist Francis Stuart.*

Blind Golf

For Helen

Even before being born we are each bound to an accord;
Our survival dependant on being linked to someone we trust.

This is how our lives evolve, whether we realise it or not.
Encountering new experiences, we become like blind golfers

Intuitively placing our faith in voices so interwoven with ours
That often we're barely conscious of their presence by our side

As we fret over club selection and outcomes, trying to fathom
Each opportunity that presents itself and every hazard to come.

The truth is that we can never navigate any course on our own.
We're not wired for solitude; our hearts must risk being blown open

Like the windborne spores of a dandelion scattered by a child's puff:
A fantasia of parachutes willingly drifting towards whatever fate intends.

So whether we call them lovers, partners, sighted-coaches or friends,
Our only certainty is our need for someone in whom to place our faith.

Read the grain of the greens for me; reassure me about how
    my ball lies,
Alert me to bunkers within my range or to what is out of bounds.

Don't tell me wind speed or direction: I feel the breeze on my cheeks:
I sense the sun, my arms tingling in anticipation of the shot to come.

I am alone in how I must execute it, yet I feel part of something bigger.
I have known disappointments, setbacks when I felt I could not go on.

All of us have been hurt by life and yet, during every round, as I must,
I slowly relearn how to open myself up and put my faith in blind trust.